# DIVERSITY, EQUALITY AND ACHIEVEMENT IN EDUCATION

# Education at SAGE

**SAGE** is a leading international publisher of journals, books, and electronic media for academic, educational, and professional markets.

Our education publishing includes:

- accessible and comprehensive texts for aspiring education professionals and practitioners looking to further their careers through continuing professional development

- inspirational advice and guidance for the classroom

- authoritative state of the art reference from the leading authors in the field

Find out more at: **www.sagepub.co.uk/education**

## Gianna Knowles and Vini Lander

# DIVERSITY, EQUALITY AND ACHIEVEMENT IN EDUCATION

**⑤SAGE**

Los Angeles | London | New Delhi
Singapore | Washington DC

First published 2011
Reprinted 2012

SAGE Publications Ltd
1 Oliver's Yard
55 City Road
London ECIY ISP

SAGE Publications Inc.
2455 Teller Road
Thousand Oaks, California 91320

SAGE Publications India Pvt Ltd
B1/I1 Mohan Cooperative Industrial Area
Mathura Road
New Delhi 110 044

SAGE Publications Asia-Pacific Pte Ltd
3 Church Street
#10-04 Samsung Hub
Singapore 049483


**Library of Congress Control Number: 2010932334**

**British Library Cataloguing in Publications data**

A catalogue record for this book is available from the British Library

ISBN 978-1-84920-600-6
ISBN 978-1-84920-601-3 (pbk)


Typeset by C&M Digitals (P) Ltd, Chennai, India
Printed and bound by CPI Group (UK) Ltd., Croydon, CR0 4YY
Printed on paper from sustainable resources

To
Kishan, Matthew, Rebecca, Simran and Tejpal
and to all children living on society's margins

# Contents

# Abbreviations and Acronyms

BME     Black and Minority Ethnic
CiC     Children in Care/Child in Care
CRT     Critical Race Theory
DAD     Disinhibited Attachment Disorder
DCSF    Department for Children, Schools and Families
DDA     Disability and Discrimination Act
DED     Disability Equality Duty
DfES    Department for Education and Skills
DfE     Department for Education
EMAS    Ethnic Minority Achievement Services
FSM     Free School Meals
GRT     Gypsy, Roma and Traveller
IND     Immigration and Nationality Directorate
Ofsted  Office for Standards in Education, Children's Services and Skills
PEP     Personal Education Plan
PSE     Personal and Social Education
RAD     Reactive Attachment Disorder
TESS    Traveller Education Support Services

# About the Authors

**Gianna Knowles** is a lecturer in Educational Studies at the University of Chichester in the UK. She has also worked with teacher trainee students from across Europe at the University of Jönköping in Sweden. Before working in higher education, Gianna gained over 12 years experience of teaching in primary schools in England, in London and the Midlands. She has worked in Local Authority Educational Advisory services, working with individual teachers and whole-school staff to develop school-wide practice and policy. Gianna has experience of being an Ofsted inspector and reviewer for the Quality Assurance Agency. Her research interest is in the area of social justice and inclusion.

**Vini Lander** is a Principal Lecturer with overall responsibility for all primary education provision at the University of Chichester. She has had experience of teaching science and working with Black and Minority Ethnic pupils and with bilingual and multilingual pupils in her time as a teacher. Vini has also been an Ofsted inspector for primary schools and initial teacher training.

Until recently she was Deputy of Multiverse, a professional resource network on achievement and diversity. As part of this role Vini has worked with tutors and student teachers across the country to help them to integrate aspects of diversity and equality into their work. As part of her wider professional role Vini has delivered training sessions to a range of education professionals on diversity, inclusion and achievement across England and in Germany.

Vini's research interests lie in the field of diversity and initial teacher education. She is undertaking doctoral research in this area.

# Introduction

## Gianna Knowles

There is a well-known poem written by Pastor Martin Niemöller in the 1930s. Many of you will know it as 'First They Came', it begins 'First they came for the Jews/And I did not speak out – because I was not a Jew'. (Niemöller, n.d.) It is a powerful poem and often cited because its seeming simplicity voices complex and challenging ideas, particularly about diversity and equality. The poem is about who individuals identify with and who they see as people who are different to them. It is also about their response to that perceived difference. The poem explores how individuals form alliances with others, especially those who seem to share similar values, attitudes and beliefs to them and how they can alienate those they perceive as being different. Part of what the poem expresses is how people may form these alliances or reject others, deliberately or unwittingly. That is, people, including ourselves, are not always aware of how our actions, or lack of actions, impact on others. The poem serves to remind us that we are, in the end, all part of the same community. Therefore, if we are looking out for others, we are also looking out for ourselves. Similarly, if we fail to support others, at some point, in times of our own need, we may find that there is no one there to support us.

These may seem challenging ideas to open this book with. The power of the poem is that while it was written at a time of significant historical events in Europe, it still remains relevant today. The poem serves to remind us that, in diverse societies such as Britain, unless we remain aware of issues such as diversity and equality, deliberate and unwitting acts of discrimination may still happen. With particular reference to this book, the poem reminds us that as adults working in schools with children with diverse needs and from diverse backgrounds, we need to be particularly mindful of our role in schools in ensuring that all children are provided for and are not discriminated against, however unwittingly.

In particular, as those concerned with children's learning, we need to consider not only that children come from diverse backgrounds, but that we also need to be proactive in recognizing the differences between children. We need to be aware of individual children's different learning needs and ensure that we are providing them with equal opportunities to learn. With regard to achievement, in terms of learning, we also need to be mindful, as Chapter 1 explores in more detail, of the link between diversity and a child's likely achievement – or underachievement in school. That is, it is part of our role to recognize and understand the diversity in our society and, as those who work with children, to respond to it in a way that enables children's achievement. We have a professional, moral and legal duty not to be culpable in allowing the diversity in our schools to lead to inequalities in educational experiences and underachievement for children.

These ideas are not new. Since 1997 schools have been successfully addressing many aspects of diversity and equality in relation to educational achievement, through developing their inclusive practice. In particular, schools have worked hard to ensure that children with specific learning needs, needs that previously might have acted as barriers to their achievement, are being taught in such a way that they are enabled to access learning effectively. Many schools are now expert at providing an inclusive education that can meet a wide range of learning needs, be they needs such as dyslexia and other cognitive learning needs, or the needs of children who are, for example, on the autistic spectrum. Schools are providing equal opportunities for children that enable them to engage in all aspects of school life and to achieve in their learning. However, as understanding about inclusion has developed, so too has the realization of the diversity and breadth of need children may bring to the classroom. For example, increasingly since the inception of the Every Child Matters (ECM) agenda, it has been understood that if equality of achievement for all is really to be realized, schools must ensure the content and delivery of the curriculum they provide for children is designed and planned with a greater understanding of the wider social context that children are part of. That is, to provide equal opportunities for children to achieve, schools need an approach to learning that also encompasses understanding about the backgrounds that children come from. Be that background in terms of culture, socio-economic status, whether the child is living with their birth family or is a Child in Care. That is to say, it is necessary to have knowledge and understanding of how the life experiences children have had, their sense of self, or identity and their current home life, impact on how they access learning. Providing equal opportunities that enable all children to achieve is about understanding the diverse families or home lives and childhoods children have, and why these need to be taken in to consideration when planning learning activities.

All those who work in the education sector are bound by legislation relating to the aspects of equality and diversity briefly outlined above, and the relevant legislation will be explored, as appropriate, throughout the book. However, depending on the role an adult holds in a school, there are also professional skills, knowledge and understanding relating to equality, diversity and achievement that they may need to demonstrate they have achieved. For example, teachers are required to *understand* how 'developmental, social, religious, ethnic, cultural and linguistic' (Training and Development Agency, 2008: 8) aspects of children's lives will impact on their engagement with their learning in schools. Teachers should also be able to take these considerations into account and 'make effective personalised provision for those they teach' (Training and Development Agency, 2008: 8). Professional development available for teaching assistants, including the achievement of Higher Level Teaching Assistant status also requires a similar understanding of these concepts. In the same way, all schools – and those working in them – are bound to consider aspects of diversity, equality and achievement as outlined in the Department for Children, Schools and Families (now the Department for Education) document (DCSF, 2007a) *Guidance on the Duty to Promote Community Cohesion*. This document states: 'the curriculum for all maintained schools should promote the spiritual, moral, cultural, mental and physical development of pupils at the school and of society' (DCSF, 2007a: 1). It goes on to say: 'schools have a duty to eliminate unlawful racial discrimination and to promote equality of opportunity and good relations between people of different groups' (DCSF, 2007a: 1). It is also worth noting here that, although the statutory curriculum in maintained schools varies depending on which country within Great Britain a school may be situated, the principles, with regard to inclusion, equality and diversity do not change. While the concepts explored in this book, and advice and guidance offered in translating understanding into action, might be discussed through particular aspects of specific curriculum documentation, the principles that underpin the ideas and practice discussed can be applied to most situations in many schools.

This introduction began by discussing how discrimination can occur because of diversity and difference. We have also seen how Britain and British schools have already made great strides in seeking to include children with diverse learning needs in their learning provision. However, the research on children's achievement shows that while there has been progress in terms of providing equality of educational opportunities for some children, particularly those who have cognitive learning needs, there are still children, who because of needs that derive from their background, continue to fail to achieve.

In seeking to explore diversity, equality and achievement in education this book begins, in Chapter 1, by discussing how our own understanding about ourselves, our own identities, values, attitudes and beliefs can impact on how we approach notions of diversity and, how those understanding then translate into our professional practice. Chapter 1 begins the exploration of the key themes relating to diversity, equality and educational achievement which will then be explored in greater depth throughout the rest of the book. In particular, the chapter examines how diversity relates to the well established inclusion agenda in schools. It introduces the link between diversity and educational achievement and underachievement and how the notion of identity is important for exploring diversity, equality and achievement.

Chapter 2 picks up the discussion about identity and diversity begun in Chapter 1 and explores the concept further. This chapter broadens the exploration of why it is important to consider identity when thinking about diversity and examines what is meant by identity. The chapter also discusses how identity can be said to be formed and may change or develop over time, depending on a person's experiences and the influences around them. The link between identity, values, attitudes and beliefs is also examined.

In Chapter 3 'Diverse Families, Diverse Childhoods', how children need to form secure attachments when young to enable them to continue to thrive, is discussed. The chapter also explores that while for many children these secure attachments are with their immediate birth family, there is still considerable diversity in what might constitute a child's 'family' and who might 'parent' a child. In the same way, the chapter considers that, just as there is diversity in terms of what might constitute a 'family', similarly there are diverse experiences of what might be termed 'childhood'. That is to say, no one family or one child may be the same as another. In relation to these ideas the chapter discusses the notion that, while of considerable significance in the raising and welfare of children, a child's immediate family is only part of the structures and systems a child interacts with to enable them to thrive. That is to say, schools too contribute to what happens to a child and their childhood and, therefore, need to consider how they respond to this aspect of their role, particularly where they work with children from a diverse range of backgrounds.

In Chapter 4, the authors explore with the reader how, over the past 50 years Britain has become an increasingly culturally diverse society. However, the term cultural diversity itself is one that can be misinterpreted and not always fully understood. Often the term is used as if it relates only to race or ethnicity. Race and ethnicity are part of what is meant by cultural diversity, but essentially it refers to the wide range of differing values, attitudes and beliefs that many groups in British society hold. Therefore, the chapter seeks to clarify the meaning and importance of the term 'ethnicity'. It discusses how, in terms of education, ethnicity and achievement are linked. It introduces the notion of whiteness, which is emerging as a concept in the literature on race and education in England, and explores how the concepts discussed in the chapter enable those who work with children to reflect on and evaluate their own position with regard to the ideas raised.

Chapter 5 discusses class as the first of the chapters of this book that begin to explore diversity and equality by looking at how the factors discussed above can impact on the achievement of particular, identifiable, groups of children and their families. In particular, the chapter discusses why class is part of the diversity, equality and achievement in education debate and what is meant by class. It explores the link between class and poverty and discusses the term 'social capital' and how it is linked to class, diversity, equality and achievement.

Chapter 6 discusses the debate surrounding boys, girls, gender issues and achievement, it acknowledges that gender is a factor that impacts on equality and achievement but also cuts across ethnicity and class. Exploration of gender issues and their impact on children's achievement at school have swung back and forth across the 'gender divide' over the past 30 years; therefore the chapter begins by exploring the salient contemporary issues related to gender and education in Britain. It sets these issues within the wider historical 'gender' framework and discusses prevailing myths about gender, seeking to provide counterarguments from recent research.

Chapter 7 'Coming from a Traveller Background: Gypsy, Roma and Traveller Children – Living on the Margins', explores the history and origins of Gypsy and Roma people and discusses the stereotypical assumptions about Gypsy, Roma and Traveller people. The chapter examines the educational debate related to children from Gypsy, Roma and Traveller heritages, discussing the difference between Gypsy, Roma and Traveller groups. The discussion also invites the reader to consider their positionality with regard to this most marginalized group of children.

Chapter 8 'Refugee and Asylum Seeker Children', explores what refugee status and asylum seeking means in terms of the law and personal experience in Britain. It discusses why people, children and families seek refuge or asylum. It explores the distinction between the terms refugee and asylum seeker and examines how the experience of refugee and asylum seeking children may impact on their learning and achievement in school, while also discussing how schools can support the well-being of refugee and asylum seeker children through understanding the wider needs of their families.

Chapter 9 discusses what it means to be a looked-after child or a Child in Care, exploring what is meant by 'looked-after' and how children come to be Children in Care (CiC). The chapter explores the role of multi-agency teams and the family courts in the process and where children go when they are looked after. The chapter discusses why CiC are particularly vulnerable to underachievement and why being looked after seems to have long-term negative impacts on a child's life chances. For example, looked-after children go on to form a disproportionate sector of the prison population. The chapter will give examples of good practice in terms of helping looked-after children to thrive and achieve.

The final chapter of the book, Chapter 10, concludes the book's exploration of diversity, equality and achievement by discussing enabling equality and achievement for children with disability. The chapter outlines what is meant by disability and the laws in Britain that schools need to be aware of, in relation to disability and working with disabled children. The chapter also explores what the barriers to learning for disabled children can be and what constitutes good practice in providing for disabled children and their families.

# 1

# Diversity, Equality and Educational Achievement

## Gianna Knowles

**This chapter explores:**

- How diversity is part of the inclusion agenda;
- The link between diversity, educational achievement and underachievement;
- How government research shows that children from diverse groups, such as minority ethnic families, deprived communities, Gypsy, Roma or Traveller families or children who are Children in Care, are among those most likely to underachieve;
- How the notion of identity is important for exploring diversity, equality and achievement.

Those of us who work with children, or who intend to work with children, know that when we are in the classroom we need to be aware of the needs of the children we are working with. However, what this chapter begins to discuss is that sometimes, unless we have had the opportunity to reflect on our backgrounds, values, attitudes and beliefs, we can unwittingly take into the classroom values, attitude and beliefs that can act as barriers to achievement for the children we work with, and actually prevent achievement occurring.

For over a decade schools have understood that children bring with them a range of learning needs. Schools have been working hard with the concept of inclusion to meet these needs and provide equal opportunities for children to achieve at school. The concept of inclusion, and the notion of inclusion in schools as it began to develop from 1997 (Knowles, 2010), is now a well embedded aspect of educational practice. All those who work in schools to enable children to enjoy and achieve, whether in their academic learning or in realizing individual potential across a range of skills and attributes, have seen the enormous benefits the inclusion agenda has brought with it (Ofsted, 2006). Schools, their staffs and the children and families who attend them, are all much more aware of the ways in which children can be engaged in enjoying and achieving at school, whatever learning needs they bring to the classroom.

 **Activity**

> Think about the range of learning needs you are aware of. These may be learning needs you have direct experience of working with in the classroom, or they may be needs you know about from your reading, talking to colleagues and through your general life experience.

Much of the initial work around the inclusion agenda focused on enabling children with learning needs – those related to cognitive learning needs as well as social and physical needs – to be included in mainstream schools. Almost all schools are far more competent now than they were 10 years ago in providing an environment that meets the needs of all children; including children with particular needs such as dyslexia, autism or a physical or sensory disability of some sort. Indeed, Ofsted in their 2006 report *Inclusion: Does it Matter Where Children are Taught?* (Ofsted, 2006) found that: 'the most important factor in determining the best outcomes for pupils with learning difficulties and disabilities (LDD) is not the type but the quality of the provision' (Ofsted, 2007: 4). They went on to state: 'there was more good and outstanding provision in resourced mainstream schools than elsewhere' (Ofsted, 2006: 4), where 'elsewhere' included special schools dedicated to catering for children with learning difficulties and disabilities. One of the central aims of the inclusion agenda is to remove the barriers to achievement in learning that some children had been identified as experiencing prior to 1997.

How children are achieving in their learning is tracked and monitored by Ofsted. To help schools improve in terms of their educational provision for children, every year, Ofsted provides information to each school about how their children are achieving against national trends and averages. The information is also broken down to show how different groups of children within the school are achieving.

That is, the information records the number of children in the school who have free school meals, special educational needs or who are 'looked-after' or are Children in Care (CiC). The information also shows how children are achieving by gender and ethnicity (Ofsted, n.d.; RAISEonline, 2010). The idea being that, through having their children's achievement reported to them in this way, schools can analyse the data and use it to further improve their educational provision. The current system for reporting this information is called: Reporting and Analysis for Improvement through School Self-Evaluation or RAISE (RAISEonline, 2010). The collecting and reporting of this achievement information has been taking place for over 10 years, it has provided invaluable information for individual schools about how they are enabling their children to achieve and improve that achievement over time.

The data has also allowed Ofsted and the government, to look at national trends with regard to achievement. The data allows comparisons to be made between how different groups of children are achieving, compared to one another. What the data has shown consistently is that some groups of children always achieve more in their learning than others. That is, the data shows there is not equal achievement between diverse groups of children. The way the children are grouped, for purposes of reporting achievement notes for each school the number of children who have a special educational need (SEN), the range of ethnicities in the school, the number of children who have free school meals, how boys and girls are achieving compared to one another and the number of children in the school who are CiC.

 **Activity**

Go back to your list of learning needs that you compiled earlier. Highlight those needs you have itemized that relate to a cognitive learning need, like dyslexia or a motor learning disability (formally known as dyspraxia), or are related to a need such as autism or a sensory or physical disability.

Now, in a different colour highlight those needs that relate to the wider social circumstances of the children. For example, children from economically deprived homes (often measured by the number of children who are eligible for free school meals – FSM), CiC, children who have a disabled parent or children who are black or minority ethnic children.

*(Continued)*

*(Continued)*

Did your list cover all the needs listed above?

Depending on your training, professional development and experience, you may find that you are more aware of the needs of some children rather than others. This book focuses on the barriers to learning for children from diverse backgrounds and will help you explore the challenges of providing equality in terms of educational opportunity for these children.

## Diversity, achievement and underachievement

Having already discussed the findings that show schools have made a positive difference in terms of achievement for children with certain learning needs, the most recent comprehensive exploration of achievement, as it relates to diversity in terms of ethnicity, shows a far less positive picture. The most recent information published by the then Department for Education and Skills, now the Department for Education (DfES, 2006a), is a document entitled: *Ethnicity and Education: The Evidence on Minority Ethnic Pupils aged 5–16.* In 2006 the DfES recorded that 21% of the children in state funded or *maintained* primary schools could be classified as belonging to a minority ethnic group (DfES, 2006a: 5). In this instance they defined the minority ethnic groups they were discussing as being:

> White Other, Black Caribbean, Black African, Black Other, Indian, Pakistani, Bangladeshi, Chinese, Mixed White & Black Caribbean and Mixed White & Black African and Chinese heritage. Where appropriate children and young people of White Irish, Gypsy/Roma and Traveller of Irish Heritage origin. (DfES, 2006a: 4)

The document also states that children from these groups 'are more likely to experience deprivation than White British pupils' (DfES, 2006a: 5). Further to this:

> Indian, Chinese, Irish and White & Asian pupils consistently have higher levels of attainment than other ethnic groups across all the Key Stages. In contrast, Gypsy/Roma, Traveller of Irish Heritage, Black, Pakistani and Bangladeshi pupils consistently have lower levels of attainment than other ethnic groups across all the Key Stages. (DfES, 2006a: 5)

The report also explores how a range of factors impact on the achievement of the ethnic minority children detailed above. For example, not only is deprivation a barrier to achievement but the report shows that children from certain ethnic groups are more likely to be excluded than others, particularly 'Gypsy/Roma, Traveller of Irish Heritage, Black Caribbean, White & Black Caribbean and Other Black pupils' (DfES 2006a: 6). It was also found that, taking other factors into consideration, 'Black Caribbean and White & Black Caribbean pupils are around 1½ times as likely to be identified as having Behavioural, Emotional and Social Difficulties as White British pupils' (DfES, 2006a: 6).

Similarly, if we explore the national statistics that report the achievement of CiC or looked-after children it can be seen that these children are not achieving as well at school as their peers. 'In 2008 only 46% of CiC achieved level 4 in English and 44% achieved level 4 in maths', whereas the national average showed that '81% of all children obtained this level in English and 79% obtained this level in maths' (DCSF, 2009h: 2).

We have seen above how the DCSF reports show that children from some backgrounds are achieving less well at school than others. On the face of it, in Britain, state education is provided free for all children. All children are taught the skills, knowledge and understanding required by statutory curriculum documentation and therefore this would seem to suggest that education provides an equal opportunity for all children and that each child, therefore, has an equal chance of achieving equally well as another child. That not all groups of children are achieving equally suggests that there are still barriers to learning occurring for some children. Some of these barriers may come from the children themselves, but we also need to consider what barriers we, as the professionals, may also be placing in children's way. We may need to consider the possibility that we, however unwittingly, may be blocking children's chances to achieve.

At the beginning of this chapter we introduced the idea that we all have personal values, attitudes and beliefs. For most of us our values, attitudes and beliefs are shaped by our own ethnicities, upbringing and experiences. Some of us may have grown up in an area which is culturally homogeneous (Tierney, 2007: 1). That is, in an area where most people seem to share the same cultural practices and beliefs.

However 'cultural diversity is an expanding social phenomenon' (Tierney, 2007: 1) and as professionals who will work in increasingly culturally diverse schools we may find that the values, attitudes and beliefs we have been used to operating with are not the same as those held by the children and families we work with. Therefore, our expectations, about the experiences, knowledge and understanding children bring to the classroom may not actually accord with those of the children and their families that we work with and this, in turn, can act as barriers to children's learning.

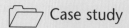 Case study

Aadila and Sally work in parallel Reception classes in a primary school in the south of England. Across their two classes are children from a diversity of social, ethnic and cultural backgrounds.

Given that the children are in Reception many of the literacy activities Aadila and Sally do with the children are based on the use of familiar stories and nursery rhymes. Using stories and rhymes for beginning reading and writing activities is recognized as good practice for Reception aged children, as the children already know orally what it is they are now seeing in print. Therefore, children can more easily make the connection between the spoken word and what it looks like written down. If they know orally the story they are now reading they can make informed decisions about unfamiliar words and use the pictures as clues as to what the text might be about.

Aadila describes herself as a British Muslim and Sally describes herself as White British with an Irish heritage. When Aadila and Sally began to work together in Reception, and discussed their planning for these activities, they very quickly realized that they shared some rhymes and stories, but that they also knew many which their colleague did not know. Talking about this they began to realize that, given the diverse nature of the classes they were working with, they could not assume all the children would share the same pool of stories and rhymes too. They felt that between them they would be able to share their own stories and rhymes with each other and with the children from similar backgrounds to themselves; however they both knew they had no knowledge of Polish stories and nursery rhymes, for example.

Aadila and Sally realized that if they were to provide all children with equal access to the learning activities they had planned, they needed to develop their knowledge and understanding of Polish nursery rhymes and traditional stories, otherwise the Polish children they were working with who had a different cultural identity to themselves may be marginalized by their belief that all the children would know the stories and rhymes they had chosen to use.

 Questions for discussion

Think about the traditional stories and nursery rhymes you know: would you say they belong to a particular cultural heritage?

Try sharing your stories and rhymes with friends from a different cultural heritage to you. What are similar about your stories and rhymes? What are different?

Thinking through the challenge Aadila and Sally have, in terms of finding stories and rhymes from a culture outside their experience, where might they go for help and support in finding the resources they need?

How could they engage the children and their families in building a resource of Polish stories and rhymes?

## Identity, diversity, equality and achievement

One of the challenging things about exploring values, attitudes and beliefs is that our values, attitudes and beliefs are elements of ourselves, closely linked to what we can consider as being our personal identity, and therefore, our very selves. Indeed the way we act and respond to what is happening in our lives we often refer to as being our 'personality'. Our understanding of our identity, who we believe ourselves to be, affects how we feel about ourselves, how we wish others to respond to us and how we present ourselves to others. Therefore, to be told that the values, attitudes and beliefs we hold may be preventing children from learning can be challenging to deal with. For example, in the case study above, Aadila and Sally knew that the stories and nursery rhymes from their backgrounds would be different to those known by some of the children they were working with. However, they also knew that using stories and nursery rhymes is one of the most successful ways of helping children begin to read. In this instance Aadila and Sally understood that to ensure that this activity could be provided equally for all children, they would need to do some research into the Polish stories and rhymes the Polish children would know. Had they used only stories and rhymes from their own backgrounds, the children from backgrounds different to that of Aadila and Sally, would have been disadvantaged.

Identity is also about belonging – we identify with others and our shared values, attitudes and beliefs are what keep us together as a family, group or community. In her writing on belonging Rachel Thompson explores how: 'Identity is about belonging, about what you have in common with some people and what differentiates you from others' (Thompson, 2007: 148). She goes on to explore how we are a complex range of possibly innate personal tendencies and the ways in which the society in which we are brought up in and live in leads us to develop, demonstrate and manage those tendencies – that is, develop an identity. However, she maintains that who we are, or present ourselves as being at any one time, and how we possibly choose to present that person or identity to others, can vary depending on the situations we are experiencing and the context we find ourselves in.

It is becoming increasingly understood that the concept of identity is fundamental to all discussions about diversity, and diversity and achievement. Again, we can see how this is manifest in the case study above. Part of Aadila's and Sally's identities are the stories and nursery rhymes they grew up with and enjoy sharing with all the children they work with. In the same way they understood that the children in their classes also have stories that are part of their identity that they too enjoy. Stories and rhymes are not only ones that can be used as good learning activities, but those which the children and their families may wish to share with others as part of who they are. Had this not been understood by Aadila and Sally then the message that would have been given to the children and their parents is that only some stories and rhymes are part of this school and, therefore, are valued by the school. This is what is meant by institutional or unwitting racism. That is, it occurs where individuals or organizations transmit messages that suggest only particular aspects of certain cultures are acknowledged and others are ignored or marginalized. Often, particularly in the field of education, this occurs because of lack of knowledge and understanding about others' values, attitudes and beliefs, rather than through acts of deliberate alienation. However, where individuals and schools fail to understand and deal with institutional or unwitting racism, particularly in the attitudes, values and beliefs of the adults that work in them and in the curriculum provided for the children, it can marginalize children and erode their sense of self, or who they identify themselves as being.

While we have explored only one instance of how assumptions about what is shared between diverse cultures can lead to inequalities in learning opportunities, for some children this example may be only one of many that happen to them throughout the school day or their life at school. In this way, the many small instances of, usually unwitting, discrimination can accumulate into a situation where children and their identities are constantly undermined. For children to whom this happens they may experience school as an alien place, leading to lack of self-esteem and disaffection. Similarly when children are unable to connect with the learning activities being provided, or are unable to access them, for whatever reasons, they are more likely to underachieve.

Let us consider another example that illustrates how we sometimes have to think beyond our immediate professional knowledge and understanding to meet the needs of the children we may be working with. PE, or physical education lessons are often ones that involve children running around, climbing and, as the name suggests, being engaged in a variety of physical activities. In some PE lessons particular skills and activities are developed and taught – gymnastic movements, dance, how to play rounders, etc. If we have a child in our PE group who is in a wheelchair, we do not expect the child to run around. Although, if we have not worked with children in wheelchairs before, it may initially be challenging for us to think of ways of planning our PE session to enable the child to be included, we would not think twice about ensuring we include the child. In the same way, we need to think about how culturally the way we are presenting our lesson activities may act as barriers to learning or present unequal learning opportunities for some of the children we are working with.

---

 ## Activity

Sometimes we are unaware of how the beliefs we carry into a classroom, the things we say and the assumptions we make about the backgrounds and experiences of the children we are working with actually impact on the children. For example, a phrase often heard in KS1 classrooms is: 'take your reading book home and read it to mum'. However, for a child who is a Child in Care or a refugee or asylum seeker child, they may not be with their mother or have any immediate contact with her.

You will be able to think of other phrases you have heard used in schools, or which were said to you as a child, that although not meant unkindly by the person saying them, show that the speaker was making assumptions about the diversity of backgrounds of the children they were working with.

---

Our outlook on life, our values, attitudes and beliefs, and our identities are formed by the people we live with and those around us, including by those we work with. Our friends have an influence on us, as does what we study and the media. However, perhaps one of the biggest influences on shaping our values, attitudes, beliefs and identity is the family that brought us up. As Parekh (2008) writes, many of us are brought up within families – however they are constituted. We try to make sense of our roles within our family units and the wider social units we operate in. We have roles in those units too as daughters, sons, siblings, parents, friends, students, employees, etc.

We take on these roles and make sense of them, in some ways we can be said to 'perform' these roles, in ways that are expected by those around us. We have been taught what we 'should' do, by those around us. We do this in ways that are worthwhile not only for ourselves, but also to please others and to ensure we have a 'place' in the wider social context we find ourselves in.

As adults we may feel fairly sure of our own identities, although we may not have given much thought to why we believe what we do, wear what we wear, eat what we eat, etc. However, if we have not reflected on the choices we have made about what we believe and the influences that have led us to these beliefs, we can fall into the trap of being blind to significant factors that impact on the achievement of the children we work with. That is to say, if we always fall back on the values, attitudes and beliefs we personally hold, at any one time, and assume they are held universally by others – or that our own values, attitudes and beliefs carry more weight than others – we can, however unwittingly, be discriminating against others.

 Case study

Louise is in her mid-20s and has muscular dystrophy. She is in a wheelchair; her sister who is two years younger, has the same condition and is in a wheelchair too. Louise says that generally growing up has been challenging and there are times when she has been very depressed. For her being a teenager was very hard. She wanted to go to discos and parties and the pub, she wanted to wear fashionable clothes and desperately wanted to have a boyfriend.

Louise says 'because of my condition I can't stand and need support in sitting up – which is why I have to have this really cumbersome wheelchair. I didn't go to a mainstream primary school, as children in wheelchairs just didn't then. However, by the time I got to 16 things began to change and my special school really supported me and my parents in getting me into a mainstream further education (FE) college. To start with it was awful, the college wasn't completely ready for wheelchair access, my tutors didn't know what to do with me. They didn't know if I could understand the work or not and I kept wanting to say 'I'm in a wheelchair, I'm not stupid'. And I was really self-conscious. I'd never been in a mainstream environment; I didn't know how to make friends. The people in my classes didn't know how to approach me. And I had all the usual teenage hang-ups about wanting to look good and go out with friends.

'Gradually things got better, although there was a lot of heartache and tears on the way. I went to university after college and again, because I was "their first student in a wheelchair" I had to go through many of the same teething problems as when I went to college. However, I was much more confident about what I could do and in knowing what to expect from others. I made great mates and did most of the "university experience". Now some of the work I do is to do with counselling children and young people with MD and talking to schools and colleges about how to support children and people like me.'

 Questions for discussion

Do you describe yourself as being disabled? How does Louise's experience compare with yours?

Do you have a friend or a family member who is disabled? Can you see any parallels with their experience and with Louise's?

Is there anything in Louise's story that surprises you or makes you think 'I hadn't thought of that'?

Is there anything about Louise's story that makes you think differently about your attitudes and beliefs about children who are disabled?

The notion of identity is explored in more detail in the next chapter, but the point to note here is that we can take very personally any suggestions that our values, attitudes and beliefs may need reflecting on, because our values, attitudes and beliefs are part of who we are. If someone challenges what we believe, they challenge us as a person. Reflecting on values, attitudes and beliefs and exploring them is not necessarily something that can happen quickly. Often such reflection takes time – time to think things through and sometimes time to research new ideas. Change, of this nature, is a process or a journey, rather than something that happens overnight. In terms of our own professional development in the area of diversity, equality and achievement we are all on different journeys and at different stages in that journey. Figure 1.1 is adapted from Adams, Bell and Griffin's (2007) notion of an action continuum. 'It describes the journey we take to better understanding of new and sometimes challenging ideas' (Knowles, 2010: 20).

## What we mean by equality and equal opportunities

As those who work with children we are well aware of the Every Child Matters (ECM) agenda and our role in enabling children and

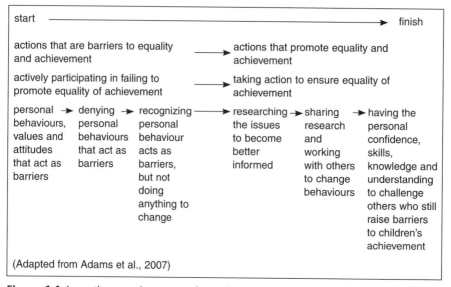

**Figure 1.1** An action continuum to show the key stages in how people's thinking and actions can change and develop

their families to achieve the five outcomes for well-being (Knowles, 2010). One of the important aspects of the ECM agenda is that the outcomes are about both the short- and the long-term. For example, if we take the first outcome, that of 'being healthy' (Knowles, 2010) we know that we can enable children to be healthy while they are at school which is a relatively controlled environment. However, the real challenge is to provide children with the knowledge and understanding that will enable them to always make healthy choices about what they eat, ensure they take physical exercise and are able to look after their mental health too, so that being healthy becomes part of their long-term identities, not just something they do at school. The ECM outcomes are quite broad in terms of what they cover and the principle that underpins them is that if these outcomes are achieved a child will enjoy well-being as they are growing up and as an adult. That is why the ECM agenda also has long-term outcomes such as requiring that children should achieve economic well-being. In this way, in working with children, we have a long-term responsibility to children to impact on their sense of self – their identities even – in terms of what they know, understand and can do to, particularly: be healthy, stay safe, enjoy and achieve, make a positive contribution and achieve economic well-being. By shaping children's attitude to the ECM outcomes we are shaping the children themselves.

One of the other principles of the ECM agenda is that the outcomes for well-being are about all children having equal entitlement to the outcomes, just as they do the skills, knowledge and understanding in the statutory curriculum documents. However, there is sometimes confusion about what this means. It is one thing to say that everyone has an equal opportunity to achieve something, it is quite another to enable those opportunities to be accessed and realized. If we consider Louise above, there are many laws and people with good intentions that support the notion that she is entitled to opportunities to achieve well-being equal to those opportunities afforded able-bodied young people.

However, equality of opportunity is not just about ensuring the opportunities are there for everyone, it is about ensuring everyone is able to access those opportunities. And sometimes, even though we have the best intentions towards the children and families we work with, because of our own beliefs we prejudice their chances in achieving the opportunities available to them. This is not to say we do this deliberately or wittingly, usually we try to help children to the best of our abilities, but sometimes because of the values, attitudes and beliefs that are so central to our own sense of self we unwittingly discriminate against others.

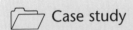 Case study

Sukhdev came to Britain from the Punjab when she was 13. While she could not speak English very well when she started at the local comprehensive school, she had been to school in the Punjab and she was very good at mathematics. However, because she was a child for whom English was an additional language the school placed her in the low ability sets for all her lessons. She was also 'withdrawn' from sessions to work with the English as an Additional Language specialist teachers for three hours per week, and she received some 'in class' support from a bilingual assistant who didn't speak Punjabi but spoke Hindi which Sukhdev knew well.

In one maths lesson where she was supported by the bilingual assistant, Sukhdev, who had finished her work, sat watching other children in the class, some of whom were not engaged with their work and were being disruptive. She turned to the bilingual assistant and said in Hindi, 'Why I am in this class with these people? I did this mathematics work when I was in primary school'. The bilingual assistant reported this back to the Head of Department who initially found it difficult to grasp that while for Sukhdev English might be an additional language, she was still good at maths. However, after some persistence by the support assistant Sukhdev was moved to a higher set for maths where she was provided with the opportunity to work at an appropriate level for her ability.

*(Continued)*

*(Continued)*

 Questions for discussion

Has anything like this ever happened to you?
How was the situation resolved?
What does this case study tell us about the school's attitude towards, and beliefs about, children for whom English is an additional language?
What might have happened to Sukhdev in terms of her self-esteem and achievement if the situation had not been resolved?
What would have been a more appropriate response to supporting Sukhdev when she first joined the school?

In this case study assumptions had been made about Sukhdev's level of mathematics based on her competence in the English language. This assumption would have affected Sukhdev's educational outcomes since in the lower set she herself was aware that she had been judged based not on her maths ability but her language ability. She was aware that she wasn't expected to achieve a lot and her placement in the lower set was affecting her well-being and self confidence.

A range of complex concepts and ideas that relate to diversity, equality and achievement in education have been raised in this chapter. It is also recognized by the authors that it is one thing to understand what is meant by diversity and difference but it is sometimes harder to know how to put this knowledge and understanding into practice in the workplace. Therefore, it is intended that the subsequent chapters of this book will provide you with the opportunity to explore more fully some of the ideas introduced here and begin to help you reflect on developing your classroom practice, to ensure you are enabling all children to enjoy and achieve at school.

## Further reading

- Adams, M., Bell, L.A. and Griffin, P. (ed.) (2007) *Teaching for Diversity and Social Justice*, 2nd edn. New York and London: Routledge.

- Department for Children, Schools and Families (DCSF) (2007) Guidance on the Duty to Promote Community Cohesion. Nottingham: DCSF.

- Department for Education and Skills (DfES) (2006) *Ethnicity and Education: The Evidence on Minority Ethnic Pupils Aged 5–16*. London: Department for Education and Skills.

- Knowles, G. (2009) *Ensuring Every Child Matters*. London: Sage.

- Ofsted (Office for Standards in Education) (2006) *Inclusion: Does it Matter Where Children are Taught?* Her Majesty's Inspectors 2535.

- Parekh, B. (2008) *A New Politics of Identity*. Basingstoke: Palgrave Macmillan.

## Useful websites

- Teacher World: http://www.teacherworld.org.uk/Articles/Robin-1.pdf
  - o For articles relating to teaching and diversity in the classroom
- Ableize: http://www.ableize.com/disabled-education/schools-and-colleges/
  - o A website owned and run by people with disabilities
- National Children's Bureau: http://www.ncb.org.uk/ecu_network
  - o Listening to children and involving them in making decisions

# 2

# Identity

## Gianna Knowles

**This chapter explores:**

- Why it is important to consider identity when discussing diversity;
- What is meant by the term identity;
- How an identity can be said to be formed and may change or
  develop over time;
- Identity, values, attitudes, beliefs.

## Identity and diversity

Diversity is about similarities and differences (Roosevelt, 2005). Britain is a society comprised of many cultures, values, attitudes and beliefs. It is also a society that acknowledges that such diversity can engender discrimination. Until recently there has been a notion that diversity, particularly in terms of differences in values, attitudes and beliefs between different groups in society, needs to be somehow reconciled into one set of beliefs and understandings for discrimination to stop. As part of the journey towards eradicating discrimination, be that racist discrimination or discrimination against people because of their gender or ability/disability, it has been increasingly understood that stopping discrimination does not mean 'everyone has to be the same'. Indeed Britain is probably a much richer and more vibrant country for acknowledging the differences that exist between people. Accepting there are differences or that diversity exists between peoples in society is not, however, the end of the story. Difference does give rise to complexity (Roosevelt, 2005) and acknowledging there is diversity means we have to acknowledge that complexity too, and, as those working with children, begin to find ways of working with that complexity in our classrooms.

One of the first ways of beginning to explore why diversity is such a complex issue is through having some insight into the link between identity and diversity, particularly through exploring how identities develop. A discussion of identity is necessary in exploring diversity, since as Hinman (2003) states: 'race, ethnicity, and culture are central to one's identity' (Hinman, 2003: 343) and identity is central to one's sense of self. This is important since when I am with those who share my race and culture I do not experience myself as being anything other than 'how people are'. My identity – the person I see myself as being – 'fits' with those around me and contributes to my sense of well-being. However, if I move into a situation where there is a diversity of races and cultures and ways of being – or identities – I may feel I 'fit' less well into this changed social situation. I may feel my values, attitudes and beliefs are challenged as is my identity and sense of self. I may feel less confident and possibly more unsure of myself.

 ## Activity

It would be unusual if, at some point in your life you had not felt that you did not share the values, attitudes and beliefs of those around you. This can happen over very small things and very often happens as we grow up and 'grow away' from people we were close to as children. In many ways, this is a part of growing-up and establishing our own identity as adults. However, sometimes, as we saw in the last chapter, the challenge to our values, attitudes and beliefs we experience as we move into different social situations can be painful and can seem to challenge our very sense of self.

Think through times when you have found aspects of your values, attitudes, beliefs or identity challenged.

What happened, how did you deal with the situation?

What impact did it have on your identity, or sense of self?

For those working or intending to work in education, exploring this link between diversity and identity is helpful in two ways. Firstly, if we have some knowledge of how identities develop we can then understand why we hold the values, attitudes and beliefs we do and why other values, attitudes and beliefs that are different to ours are just as strongly held by others. In terms of working in the classroom, we can also begin to understand how our identities impact on our approach to our role in the classroom and why, if our attitudes, values and beliefs are different to those experienced by the children we teach, we may unwittingly be preventing children from achieving in their learning.

Secondly, exploring identity allows us to understand how values, attitudes and beliefs are fundamental to our sense of self. This, in turn, can mean that as professionals we may find it hard to 'change our minds' about things, even when we know the evidence before us suggests we should. For example, as Dr Barbara Thompson (Thompson in Knowles, 2006) discusses, prior to the Sex Discrimination Act 1975 the values, attitudes and beliefs about education for girls that were widely held by teachers and others were ones that centred on the importance of preparing girls for being wives and mothers; which, at the time, was a culturally dominant notion about the role of girls and women. For these reasons the Norwood Report argued that: 'the grounds for including domestic subjects in the curricular are ... firstly that knowledge of such subjects is necessary equipment for all girls as potential makers of homes' (Thompson, 2006: 95). However, now we believe that being homemakers is only part of what girls and women might want for themselves, or be potentially capable of. It has also been the case that this change in the dominant values, attitudes and beliefs about how and what girls should be enabled to attain at school has taken decades and acts of parliament to achieve. Further to this, throughout this time of change, both men and women in education, and wider society, were resistant to new ideas about educating girls, even when they knew girls were capable of so much more than they were being offered. That is to say, even in the face of quite compelling evidence people can still be resistant to giving up values, attitudes and beliefs they hold, particularly if they feel that giving them up may also mean losing some of what they see as being their identity. For example, some researchers still claim that while girls and women may now benefit from greater opportunities, this has been at the expense of boys and men losing aspects of their role in society (Braudy, 2005; Litosseliti, 2002; Reumann, 2005).

## What do we mean by identity?

In thinking about personal or individual identity we can be said to be thinking about two interrelated aspects. One is the physical dimension of the object or person in question and the other is bound up with the psychological aspects of being that person (Garrett, 1998: 41). It is also possible to argue that both physical and psychological aspects can change and vary over time. Most obviously certain physical characteristics can change considerably over time; we change physically in many ways throughout our lives, from the moment we are born, through childhood, adolescence, into middle and old age. Some of these changes are beyond our control although increasingly we can have a direct impact on our physical appearance. We can modify our weight and change aspects of our appearance through surgery and the way we dress. We may suffer accidents that will alter our appearance. But in terms of our psychological characteristics to what extent are we determined by our biological make-up and to what extent is our identity – who we and others believe us to be – under our conscious control? Is it possible that we could change our physical and presenting psychological selves to such an extent that someone who had not seen us for a number of years would be unable to recognize us? But would we have really changed internally or are we just choosing to show different parts of ourselves?

In many ways it is our psychological selves or identities that we often regard as being our true identities, since human beings will often claim to have a core self that continues, unchanged, throughout our lives. Indeed, when we work with children we very often talk about helping them 'realize' this 'self'. That is, we may change our approach to and opinions about things, but our sense of who we fundamentally are continues and survives by making sense of the experiences we engage with and the memories we hold, storing information in response to those inputs, sometimes revising that information and acting on how that information and those memories add to our knowledge of ourselves, and our values, attitudes and cultural understandings (Garrett, 1998: 42).

This interest in trying to explain the psychological aspect of human identity has been one that has interested people throughout time, however in Europe one of the most influential thinkers in this area was Sigmund Freud. At the end of the nineteenth century Freud began to develop a theory that sought to explain how our psychological identity develops in response to how our subconscious, impacted on by the wider social context around us, reconciles tensions within our growing psychological selves. For Freud we begin as infants driven by physiological needs that are necessary for our survival as helpless, vulnerable infants.

> The 'pleasure principle' is what governs us at birth and this principle pushes us towards the instant gratification of all our wishes. As we grow up and discover that we have to live with, and adapt to, the natural world and other people, the 'reality principle' comes into operation. (Rennison, 2001: 31)

If we grow up in a supportive environment with significant others around us who are concerned about our welfare – in the broadest sense – then we learn to manage this basic desire in socially acceptable ways, depending on the cultural norms we are being brought up with. That is, at this period in our lives and arguably throughout our lives, we need appropriate significant others around us who help us reconcile our wants with the demands of our wider social context. This notion of significant others will be further explored in Chapter 3.

Freud called the part of us that can be wholly selfish and wants instant gratification the id. The id is a necessary part of a baby's survival mechanism since it drives the baby to cry for food, warmth and comfort. However, for humans to live in a social context they need to learn to manage the gratification of these immediate basic needs and reconcile them with the needs and desires of others. Freud called the rational part of the mind, the part that reacts to the outside world and allows the individual to adapt to reality, to acknowledge the 'reality principle' (Rennison, 2001: 39), the ego. For Freud there was also the superego that is: 'the internalised voice of parents, carers and society which provide the individual with the rules and regulations that guide it when it moves beyond primary narcissism' (Rennison, 2001: 39). This basic premise of Freud's theory has had a profound impact on the way Europe and the West regards the notion of psychological identity, particularly when it comes to exploring how values, attitudes and cultural notions that have become part of our identity develops and can change.

Lawler (2009) however also considers to what extent identity is influenced by our genetic heritage and to what extent it is a product of the wider influences of our environment. If who we are, our dispositions to behave in certain ways and present ourselves to others in certain ways, is determined by our DNA, we might seem to be 'at the mercy' of our genes and have little or no control over who we are. Or is it, as Freud suggests, that who we are may to a greater extent be determined by our upbringing and environment? It may be that both genes or nature – and our social context or nurture – have an impact on our identity. However, if as Freud claims we can be said, at whatever level, to be shaped by external experiences, then we can also choose to allow some of those influences to have more impact on us than others. That is, we may have some control in what Lawler (2009) terms 'achieving our identity'. That is to say, that although our identity may have an essential basis stemming from our genes, it could be argued that these provide us with the raw materials from which an identity can be constructed.

We do, however, often behave as if we have some determination over our identity as we say things like 'I wouldn't normally choose to wear these clothes, but I have to for work, they aren't really me'. In our leisure time, we seek out places, pursuits and friends that allow us to relax and 'be ourselves'. That we know we are 'different' depending on the place we are in and the people we are with raises ideas about identity that need to be pursued further.

If we do believe we are 'different' depending on circumstances, then this would suggest that we have some notion of being in control of our identity and so may also have, to varying extents, control over the impact others make on us. In this way the term identity is linked to the other, that is part of having an identity is about identifying with, or refusing to identify with others. The term *identify* suggests an action, we identify ourselves with something outside ourselves, including with others. And, by reciprocation, those things and others we identify with will determine aspects of our identity. Therefore, we might, as part of our identity, say we are male, or female or transgender, we might then go on to further identify ourselves as identifying with particular groups within that broader category, so as a woman we may also want to identify ourselves as being 'single' or 'a mother'. In the same way as we may identify with sub-groups within the wider category, we may also be 'dis-identifying from certain features of being' in that category that we find 'unattractive or unpalatable' (Lawler, 2009: 2). In this way we can identify ourselves as being part of wider socially recognized and defined categories but we can also show how we are different to others within these categories. There may be groups in society that we do not want to identify with and we will seek to ensure that, possibly by our outward appearance and certainly through the values, attitudes and beliefs we hold, that we cannot be identified with those groups.

---

 Activity

Think about how you describe yourself in terms of gender. That is, do you think of yourself as being male, female or transgender?

Thinking about the portrayal of male, female and transgender people in the media, who do you identify with and who do you seek to be different from?

What is it that you do to show your similarity to others with whom you identify – for example, is it in the way you dress, the values, attitudes and beliefs you hold, your aspirations and the way you live your life?

What is it that you do that shows you do not identify with other people and personalities portrayed in the media?

By making these distinctions, what is it that you want people to know you have in common with these others – what aspects of them do you want to be seen as sharing? And where you believe you are different from others what aspects of them do you want to be seen as rejecting?

## Producing an identity

Sometimes the formation of an identity can be seen as being a product of the narrative, or story, of our lives. In our personal reflections about 'ourselves' or 'who we are' and when involved in 'explaining ourselves' to others we will often set our current 'selves' in a wider narrative of 'our lives'.

 Activity

On a large piece of paper and with some coloured pens, draw a road map through your life. Chart those people and events that you feel have had a significant impact on your identity.

As with all narratives there are main characters, minor characters, main plots and sub-plots. There are also those incidental events or chance meetings with others which, later in the narrative, turn out to be significant. Or there are characters that return to the narrative and completely change the direction that things seemed to be going in. There are also random and unforeseen events that impact on our narratives, some very exciting – and some very tragic.

One of the aspects of our narratives to consider is that, however personal we believe our narrative to be, they are constructed in relation to the narratives of others. That is, those who feature in our stories have their own stories too and these may also have had an impact on our narratives, and, just as our narratives are shaped by other people, will we shape theirs. Wider social events will also significantly impact on personal narratives – war, recession and dominant discourses.

## Activity

Go back to your map of your life and draw in someone else's narrative. Also mark in where external events impacted on you – or ideas that were, or are, prevalent in wider society at any one time.

## Case study

Janice and Paul were at school together, at one point Paul asked Janice if she would like to go and see a film with him. Janice said 'no' and in discussing this time in her relationship with Paul she says we were quite good friends, but 'there was something which made "going out" together a non-starter'.

Immediately after school they moved away from the area and lost touch. Then, one evening a few years later, quite by accident, Janice walked into a pub she had never been in before. Having bought a drink, sat down and looked around she realized that most of the people in the pub were gay. And, there was Paul. After the surprise and delight of seeing each other after so long, and Janice explaining she was there 'by accident' and Paul explaining he definitely meant to be there, they spent some time 'catching-up' on each other's news. Paul said he was doing chemistry at university and hating it, but that having come out he had set about changing many things in his life. He was going to finish his course and get his degree, but he had also taken up dance and was training to be a dancer. Janice and Paul remained in touch for a few years and were much closer friends than they had been at school, in part because Paul was much happier and had a much stronger sense of 'self' and they were able to have a relationship that was not confused by feeling that the only relationship that they could have was one of girlfriend and boyfriend.

## Questions for discussion

What pressures do you think Paul might have experienced at school that made him try to conform to a dominant view of how he should behave?

Do you think Paul should have tried harder to conform, or that he was right to do what he did and be true to his own sense of self?

Have you even been in a situation where you felt you were denying your identity?

We may believe we have choices in forming our personal identity, but often we may be compromising more than we think because of dominant discourses that exist in wider society. Indeed significant parts of what we see as aspects of ourselves that we have deliberately cultivated may actually have been scripted for us. Most notably over the last century we can see this in how we are expected to behave in relation to our gender. For example, throughout the twentieth century the role society expected women and men to fulfil changed considerably. As Parekh (2008: 16) states: 'Every society has a more or less well-articulated system of identities, each subject to certain norms, carrying certain privileges or privations, and enforced by formal or informal sanctions that form part of its disciplinary regime'.

Further to this, as Parekh also explores how dominant aspects of society such as the media, community leaders and often central government will seek 'to ensure that its members not only conform to but internalize their social identities, that is; identify themselves with and internalize the norms of these identities' (Parekh, 2008: 16). That is to say, those in power believe they have more to lose by challenging these notions that impact on identity, rather than examining them to see if as concepts they actually confine the possible ways in which someone's identity might develop, given more freedom and choice. Recognized and accepted societal identities seemingly provide order and stability for a society. Indeed, there can be freedom in certainty. However: 'they can also take us over and become prisons' (Parekh, 2008: 16). There can also be dominant identities which marginalize others, since social identities represent a particular way of seeing the world and behaving in the wider social context. 'Identities do not co-exist passively' (Parekh, 2008: 24), they impact on one another. Children quickly 'pick-up' those identities which are expected of them and learn how to 'perform' that identity.

 Case study

Amy (5) says, 'when I am at school I'm allowed to play outside on the scooters, I like to splosh my feet in the puddle to make it go fast. When I'm at home my mum says – "you can't go out in this rain", I think she doesn't want me to get dirty'.

Aanand (10) says, 'when I was at nursery I remember pretending to be my sister Sai. I used to dress-up in a red sari they had and

*(Continued)*

*(Continued)*

pretend I was making chapatis for everyone. I used to think making chapatis always looked like a great thing to do, but my dad said it was women's work'.

 Questions for discussion

Why does Amy's mum want Amy to stay clean and tidy?
Why does Aanand's father react as he does to Aanand playing at cooking?
What values, attitudes and beliefs might Amy and Aanand take on board because of their parents' behaviour?
Do you think Amy's mother's behaviour and Aanand's father's behaviour will impact on their children's developing identity?

## How we deal with the identity of others

Having thought about our own identities let us now look at how we seek to live alongside others and their identities. By exploring what our own identities may be comprised of and looking at the complexity of our own selves we must also know that others have the same complex structures that they too are working with, or are the product of. However, often, when we are thinking about others this does not seem to be part of our reasoning. Pennington (2000) in writing about our social selves – us dealing with others, rather than us dealing with ourselves – suggests that while we work very closely with our own narratives in seeking to realize who we are and explain ourselves to others, we can be very dismissive of the same process in others. Therefore, in working with children, it is important to understand that they do not come to school as entities separate from their home background and community. Children, as young human beings who are still in the early stages of forming, performing and understanding themselves, will be part of an almost a seamless whole with their background. For these reasons, to ensure schools are providing learning opportunities that meet the needs of children from a diversity of backgrounds they need to understand and work with the child's family and community, if the learning presented is to be meaningful to the child. That we are part of a wider whole and that this 'whole' impacts consciously or subconsciously on us is a concept that is also explored by Parekh (2008). For Parekh: 'every social identity links us to a particular group of people, makes us part of a historical narrative, and gives our lives a meaning and depth' (Parekh, 2008: 24). However, he also acknowledges that the notion we have of ourselves is complex and, often multi-layered since we will have 'multiple belongings, loyalties and sources of meaning' that enable us 'to construct several overlapping narratives of our lives' (Parekh, 2008: 24).

The idea of *multiple belongings* is, in a diverse society, an important aspect of identity to consider. In a mono-cultural society it may be arguable that, in terms of identity we have fewer loyalties or sources of meaning we need to consider in terms of defining ourselves. For most of us, however, we have multiple belongings, we are sons or daughters, we may be parents, we are friends, students, employees, etc. At any one time we may need to prioritize one narrative of our lives above others depending on the situation we are in. For example, when we are in the classroom we may be focusing on an aspect of our identity and narrative of our lives that requires different things from us to when we are out with friends. How often will people who know us, on seeing us in situations where we do not usually meet them say 'I did not recognize you at first', or 'I did not know you could do that'.

## 🗁 Case study

'I am a British Muslim. I was born in Britain and my parents are from Iran. I say I am a British Muslim since I love living in Britain and enjoy all the things about Britain my non-Muslim friends do, but being a Muslim is also very important to me. It is part of my identity. With all the talk about terrorism, particularly since the July bombings in London in 2007, I sometimes get scared. Some people think because I am a Muslim I am automatically a terrorist, or agree with the terrorists. At the time there were fights at school about it too and lots of racist name calling. But I am just as scared by the thought of terror attacks as anyone.'

'I don't wear a hijab – a scarf over my hair and neck – probably because my mother doesn't. She says when she lived in Iran in the 1960s women didn't wear them; it was enough that they dressed modestly, which she does. My older sister has decided to wear one and some of my friends do. When we are out in London, no one seems to care or notice, but when we have been on visits to friends outside London I have been quite shocked by how people have stared at my sister – sometimes they giggle and you can see them nudging their friends. Sometimes you can see people actually backing away. I want to tell them this is part of who my sister is, it does not make her an alien or a terrorist, she pays her taxes and contributes to Britain.'

*(Continued)*

*(Continued)*

 Questions for discussion

Firstly, think about the speaker in the case study, she talks about a range of complex and sometimes conflicting tensions in her life – that is, the multi-layered aspects of her life, all of which are linked to her identity. Although we may experience life differently to the person talking here, many of us also have multi-layers to our lives that we need to learn to manage to preserve our own identities. Do you have examples of how you have had to balance complex aspects of your life to keep your identity whole?

Secondly, if you met the speaker in this case study and she told us about her experiences, how would you respond? Would you, for example, have similar experiences to share with her? Or is the multi-layering of your life very different – in which case how could you help her to understand your identity?

Unless we are aware of this notion of multiplicity and layering that is part of people's identities, Pennington (2000) suggests that we can tend to use aspects of our own identity and transfer them onto others. This means we are making judgements based on examples of our dispositions to behave in one way or another, as opposed to verifiable situational factors. Pennington (2000) calls this false consensus and this notion can be used to explain why the behaviour of others can surprise or shock us, that is, we expect everyone's reaction to particular events to be the same as our reaction. Pennington (2000) suggests that there are three possible explanations for the 'false consensus effect' (Pennington, 2000: 47). Firstly because many of our social interactions with friends, family and partners are likely to be with people who do have views similar to us we can often assume that these values, attitudes and beliefs are more widespread than they actually are. Secondly, because what we believe and our thoughts are all consuming for us, we can have a tendency to believe that our concerns are also the concerns of others. The third part of the false consensus concept is that 'motivation and our own self-esteem may have a role to play in that our own self-esteem may be enhanced by believing that other people hold the same opinions as ourselves' (Pennington, 2000: 47).

A further interesting point to note about the false consensus effect is that it can lead to what Pennington describes is 'defensive attributional bias' (2000: 55). That is, not only do we attribute our own values, attitudes and beliefs to others but we can also 'take sides' with those who do hold the same values, attitudes and beliefs so as to defend our beliefs or deny that any aspect of what we believe might be open to question. For example, in the previous case study Paul may have known he was gay when he was at school, but the prevailing values, attitudes and beliefs at that school in the late 1970s were ones that were hostile to homosexuality. Those around Paul assumed everyone was straight and not only that, but that it was a bad and *unnatural* thing to be gay. Those around Paul worked together, whether consciously or unconsciously, as a group to defend their own and others' biased attitudes to protect their own identities, values and beliefs even if it meant denying Paul his identity. Such defensive behaviours from groups of people who share similar values, attitudes and beliefs and are confronted by other ways to live life and other identities can be seen all around. Pennington (2000) cites the example of 'conservatives in the United States who thought that poor people were more personally responsible for their plight and could do more to avoid poverty' than they claimed (Pennington, 2000: 54).

Not only do we have the capacity to identify and work with like-minded people to defend our values, attitudes and beliefs but we will also be prepared to be more tolerant and understanding of the behaviour of those we identify with. Of course, there is no problem with this laissez-faire approach unless the behaviour of others could be called into question and this may happen in our professional lives in terms of promoting equality for the diverse children we work with. I may feel fairly secure with the part of my identity linked to being tolerant and treating people equally; I may feel I have no particular prejudices or unwitting aspects to my personality and beliefs that get in the way of enabling all children to achieve at school, however, if I am surrounded by people who think the same as me, how would I know? I may find out more about my own attitudinal biases by reflecting on situations which make me react defensively and negatively towards those who say and do things I disagree with. Often we do not reflect on values, attitudes and beliefs or other aspects of our identity unless there is something external to us that prompts us to do so (Pennington, 2000). Considerations about our health might motivate us to change our views on how much exercise we take. Similarly in our working lives we sometimes come upon situations that require us to reflect on the values, attitudes and beliefs we hold.

As we explored in Chapter 1, reflecting on our own values, deciding which to keep and which to modify in the light of new ideas and new information is both part of our professional development and part of living in a diverse society. Elias (2001) states: 'social patterns of self-regulation which the individual has to develop within himself or herself in growing up into a unique individual, is generation-specific and thus, in the broader sense, society-specific' (Elias, 2001: viii). Essentially, what Elias is suggesting is that each generation has to invent itself and reinterpret its values, attitudes and beliefs so they work for that generation. Society is forever changing, both in terms of who and what comprises that society, and under the impact that technological change and wider global events such as war and natural disasters have on that society. The cultural diversity of Britain has changed considerably since 1945 and we can see by how people identify themselves in terms of their ethnicity and cultural background that, as a society, we are beginning to identify what we have in common, as well as those things that are different between the diverse groups in Britain.

The subsequent chapters of this book will develop further some of the ideas introduced here. The main aim of this chapter has been to raise with you the notion that our identity – where we have come from and where we see ourselves as going, both psychologically and socially – may impact on how we respond to the issues relating to diversity and equality discussed in this book.

## Further reading 📖

- Bird, C. (1999) *The Myth of Liberal Individualism*. Cambridge: Cambridge University Press.

- Daiute, C. (ed.) (2006) *International Perspectives on Youth Conflict and Development*. Oxford: Oxford University Press.

- Du Gay, P. (ed.) (1997) *Production of Culture/Cultures of Production*. London: Sage/ The Open University.

- Elias, N. (2001) *The Society of Individuals*. New York and London: Continuum International Publishing.

- Parekh, B. (2008) *A New Politics of Identity*. Basingstoke: Palgrave Macmillan.

## Useful websites 🖱

- Theory: http://www.theory.org.uk

  o A website that explores materials on media and identity, collected by David Gauntlett, Professor of Media and Communications at the University of Westminster

- *Self and Identity*: http://www.tandf.co.uk/journals/titles/15298868.asp

  o This is the website link for the journal *Self and Identity*

# Diverse Families, Diverse Childhoods

## Gianna Knowles

---

**This chapter explores:**

- How children need to form secure attachments when young to enable them to thrive;
- That for many children these secure attachments are with their immediate birth family, however, there is considerable diversity in what might constitute a child's 'family';
- The notion that a child's immediate family is only part of the structures and systems a child interacts with to enable them to thrive;
- What we mean by parenting.

---

In the previous chapter we explored how understanding the concept of identity is an important part of working with children from diverse backgrounds. The exploration of identity also considered how important families are in how identities develop and are maintained. This chapter picks up and further discusses the notion of families, family diversity and family and identity. The chapter is also concerned to explore the notion of family and that of childhood since much of the work primary schools are engaged in is closely linked with children's families. Therefore, if we are to understand how to provide equality of opportunity for the diverse needs of the children we work with, we need also to understand how our understanding of family, family diversity and diversity in experiences of childhoods impact on our work.

Activity

In previous activities you have been asked to think about friends, family and others who have helped shape your identity and the person you feel you are. Similarly, you have considered how you have impacted on their story too.

The terms 'family' and 'childhood' can be terms that conjure up very definite ideas about what a 'family' should be, who a person's family is and how a family should operate. Similarly, when we think of 'childhood', we can have strong views on what 'being a child' is about: the things children can, or cannot, do; or the things they should, or should not do.

Either by yourself or with friends reflect on who you regard as your family. How many of the people you have thought of are you related to? Have the people you regard as family changed as you have grown up, you have met a partner's family or you have lost some of your family members? Are the people you rely on most related to you, or are they friends? Does your experience of family reflect that of your friends?

The likelihood is that no two people will have the same experience of 'family'. Keep this thought in mind as you read this chapter, since although we know families are diverse and, therefore, so are child-hoods, schools can sometimes behave as if all children have the same experience of families and of being a child.

## Attachment

When exploring the concepts of families and childhood, attachment is an important concept to consider, for two reasons. Firstly, attachment, as outlined in this chapter, explains not only why families are so important to the flourishing of children, but also secondly, that it does not matter how a child's family is constituted, having a family to attach to, however 'diverse' that family might be, is what is important for a child to thrive.

The most important things children need to thrive and flourish are capable, loving and caring people around them with whom they can form mutually supportive attachments (Mayseless, 2002; Prior, 2006). The notion of attachment and caregiving as expressed in this way comes from the work of John Bowlby in the 1960s and 70s. In the way Bowlby uses the term attachment he is referring to the tie or bond a child forms with those who are its primary caregivers. Attachment bonds are initially formed because of the survival needs infant human beings have; the need for food, shelter and security. Most such bonds also develop into one of considerable mutual love, care and affection. However, in Bowlby's use of the term attachment, he is referring to an instinctive attachment that develops because of the infant human's need to attach to a caregiver who will ensure its survival, in the most basic sense (Prior, 2006: 15). In the same way, Bowlby refers to the person with whom the infant forms these primary attachments to as the caregiver (Prior, 2006: 15; Mayseless, 2002). From the infant's point of view, they will instinctively manifest their need for food or security, or release from whatever sense of discomfort they are experiencing, to whoever seems to provide relief (Oppenheim, 2007; Prior, 2006: 17). Over time, as the attachment bond develops the infant will come to know what behaviours are most likely to produce the relief from discomfort wanted from the caregiver. As the infant grows and develops they will be able to discriminate between caregivers around them and understand the behaviour likely to produce desired responses from them (Oppenheim 2007; Prior, 2006: 16). Then, between the ages of two or three the infant – now a young child – can begin to see their primary caregiver as a person separate from themselves and the relationship will develop into a more complex relationship or *partnership* (Prior, 2006: 16).

While Bowlby acknowledges that we continue to form attachments and be attached to others throughout our lives. After the age of two or three, when we can see others as people other to ourselves with their own desires and motivations, we continue to have attachments, but not in the same way as we do as infants. As children become young people their attachment to those who were of primary importance in childhood begin to be overtaken by friends and, as they become young adults, by more intimate partnerships.

In his early work Bowlby centred much of his theory on the attachment/caregiver bond between mother and child. The implication seemed to be, that for children to form appropriate early attachments that would enable them to thrive as infants and later as young children moving out into the wider world and needing to form attachments with others, it was the child's mother who had to be the primary figure the child attached too. However, Bowlby's later work states that infants are able to form attachments to more than one caregiver and that successful attachment figures do not have to be the child's mother. Indeed an infant 'can have more than one attachment figure and often has several' (Prior, 2006: 56). What is of paramount importance to the child's likelihood of thriving is that the caregivers are there not only to meet the basic survival needs the infant has, but that they are also sensitive to wider needs the child has, because of the nature of them as individuals, but also in terms of providing the wider aspects of care and nurturing we know children need to thrive. Prior (2006) also suggests that of primary importance for children is: 'safety, protection and sense of security' (Prior, 2006: 58). Prior acknowledges that love and care usually develop from these bonds, however, for Prior 'the child's first need is for safety. A loved child who is unsafe is in physical and psychological peril. Love alone is insufficient' (Prior, 2006: 58). In the same way, while love alone is not enough to ensure a child thrives, so too caregiving which lacks affection and is purely instrumental in terms of providing for physical needs and fails to provide for emotional needs, may cause a child to grow up feeling unwanted and with low self-esteem.

## The child in the wider social context

The work of Bowlby was, and remains, central to our understanding of how important it is for children to be able to form secure attachments from birth, with those who will be able to provide the infant and young child with the care they need. While Bowlby claims that the initial bond between the baby and its caregivers, is based on the infant's innate biological drive to ensure it has its basic needs met, for most children and their caregivers, this is usually a relationship which includes much mutual affection. Chapter 8 explores the emotional and physical impact on children who do not establish a secure and flourishing bond with a caregiver or caregivers. These may be children whose caregivers cannot, for whatever reasons, provide the necessary care and affection for the infant. Or, it may be that because of bereavement or parental separation the child suffers the loss of one or more of their caregivers. In such cases children may become looked after children, or Children in Care (CiC).

Where a child is a CiC, society, usually through agents such as social workers, have needed to 'step in' to try and provide a more secure environment for a child to grow up in than the one they have been living in, that is, to provide some form of surrogate family.

In Chapter 2 we explored how an individual's identity is formed in the early years of life. The chapter discussed how we may have innate characteristics that drive how our identity develops while immediate external influences from those around us and our environment will also impact on a developing identity. In the late 1970s the psychologist Urie Bronfenbrenner began to explore how human beings are essentially social beings who, from an early age, live in a social environment which will impact on their developing selves. For Bronfenbrenner, aspects of the way we learn to behave as children, and traits which can be said to form our identity, are rooted in and reflect the social context in which they developed (Dunlop, 2006: 159).

## Bronfenbrenner's ecological environment model

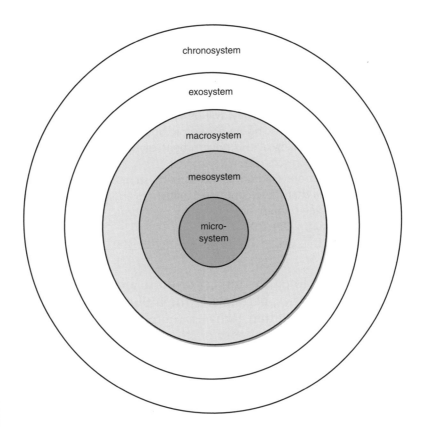

If we imagine a set of concentric circles, as shown in the figure above, in the middle Bronfenbrenner places the child in what he terms the 'microsystem'. The microsystem also includes those primary caregivers who are the first people the infant will bond with. The microsystem will, therefore, include parents, siblings and others close to the infant from birth and in the first few months and years of the child's life.

Moving out from this central circle into the next circle Bronfenbrenner describes the child as moving out into wider society and into the mesosystem. The mesosystem is the bridge between the home, or microsystem, and environments the growing child will move into such as school and the circle of friends the child will develop.

If we continue to move out through our concentric circles we move from the mesosystem to the macrosystem. The macrosystem explores

*(Continued)*

*(Continued)*

those influences on a child which occur: 'indirectly through the parents, siblings, or friends. Stress in the parent's workplace and its effects on parenting are an example' (Deater-Deckard, 2004: 116). The next circle in our conceptual model is the exosystem. The exosystem contains the wider aspects of the society which the child grows up in that will have an influence on the developing child, but the immediate links between the individual and the influences may sometimes seem very intangible or indirect. For example, the aspects of the exosystem that will impact on the child, positively or negatively, will be whether the society the child is growing up in is experiencing an economic boom, or a recession. It will also contain the policies of the government of the time, fashions and prevailing dominant discourses.

The final circle in our diagram is the chronosystem. 'The chronosystem represents the idea that these contextual influences and all of the complex connections between them are changing over time' (Deater-Deckard, 2004: 116; Empson, 2004: 30).

Having already explored the impact of those around us on the formation of our identities, particularly the influence of those around us when we were children, what is helpful about the work of Bronfenbrenner is that his theory explores the impact of wider societal influences on the development of individuals and identity. It is sometimes tempting to think of children as growing up in a bubble, where they are protected from the wider complexities of the adult world. However, if Bronfenbrenner is correct in what he suggests his model shows how children are directly and indirectly affected by wider issues and events happening around them. Robb (2001) also states that childhood is a time dominated by adults who, to a greater extent, control most of what happens for a child – from choosing the clothes a child wears, the food they eat, what they watch on television to the friends they should play with and the school they should go to. There can also be a tendency on the part of adults to behave as if the current generation of children are ungrateful for not realizing how much better things are for them, particularly in material terms, than they were for their parent's generation. Robb (2001) writes that the picture of childhood in Britain can be experienced as 'a stereotyped picture of modern children as spoilt and over-materialistic' (Robb, 2001: 19). However, as he also points out, children learn their behaviour from those around them and if the adults are using material objects to define themselves and establish their sense of identity and status, children will learn to do this too. Further to this Robb (2001) also reminds us that there is considerable money to be made from children and 'childhood'. There are a number of industries whose livelihood is dependent on children: the toy industry, the section of the media that caters for children – advertising, fashion, entertainment, films – as well as leisure pursuits, including the 'traditional' dancing lessons, horse riding, swimming and football. It is only adults who believe children are unaffected by the wider workings of the world.

---

 Activity

In his ecological environment model Bronfenbrenner explores the impact of wider social events on the development of the child. Think back through your life, can you find any examples of how events in wider society directly – or indirectly – impacted on your childhood and possibly your developing sense of self? These may be events that had a positive or negative impact, they may be huge societal events such as wars or lighter trends such as a particular music fashion. The impact may have been fleeting in terms of the effect it has had on you, or you may still be living with the lasting consequences of these events. If you are still unsure what Bronfenbrenner is exploring through his notion of the ecosystem and chronosystem, read the case studies below to help your thinking.

---

 Case studies

Innocence was born in Jamaica and, at the age of 12 came to Britain with her parents in 1951. She says: 'My father had been in the RAF in the war and was stationed in Britain. He said we would like it here and he'd fought for "the mother country" so people would welcome us. When we got here we arrived in a country still recovering from the war. London was like a bomb site and there was still rationing. While the white British were happy for black Jamaicans to fight in the war for them, they weren't quite so welcoming now everyone was scrabbling to make a living.'

'Finding somewhere to live was hard too. It was just like that sign they show sometimes on TV documentaries about the time, you know the one: "no blacks, no Irish, no dogs".'

'My name is Rebecca and I'm now in my late 40s, but I was in my 20s in the 1980s and had just started work. Britain really seemed to have found itself and was booming. Work was so easy to find and it was a great time and a great time for young women. My friend

*(Continued)*

*(Continued)*

and I bought ourselves suits – with the shoulder pads and everything. We really thought we could do anything and go anywhere. I still look back on those days as being some of the happiest times of my life. Things seem so much harder for my own daughter, you have to have qualifications to do everything now, I don't know how she's going to afford to buy a house and get a mortgage. You think things are always going to get better, but it's not always like that. Mind you, she is going to university which is something that wasn't there for me.'

Atorena says: 'I am 12 and living in Britain with my grandparents and my sister. I come from Baghdad in Iraq. When the British and American bombing started in 2003 my mother took us to Saudi Arabia to stay with my aunt. My mother went back to Baghdad to be with my father and they are still there. My aunt brought us to Britain so we could be safe and looked after by our grandparents. Our flat is quite small and I share a bed with my sister. I was very homesick when I first came and really missed my parents – I haven't seen them since 2003. When it is better in Baghdad I want to go back and see them, but I might come back to Britain again as this is what I know now.'

'My name is Sam, I'm nine and in Year 4 at school. I really like school, I have lots of friends and we play football at lunchtime. I'm good at football and play in a team at the weekend. I'm quite good at maths too and like using the computers at school. I like it when the teacher does stuff on the interactive whiteboard and we get to use it. We're doing about the environment at the moment. Sometimes it does worry me about what's going to happen, I worry about the [polar] bears whose ice sheets are melting. Sometimes I think, I'll be an adult soon and have to sort all these problems out.'

 Questions for discussion

Go back to each of the case studies above and see if you can iden-tify how particular social and political events impacted on what the speakers are saying?
Think of your own life and particularly your childhood. As you reflect on it now can you see how wider events have had an impact on shaping your life?
Think about social and political events now, how might they be shaping the lives of the children you are working with?

Bronfenbrenner's model is also helpful in that it enables us to explore how aspects of inequality work at a societal level. While those who work with children in schools – which in Bronfenbrenner's model is part of the mesosystem – seek to provide equality of opportunity for children because of the other factors operating in the mesosystem, exosystem and chronosystem, the success school can achieve for children, in terms of equality and achievement, may be diluted by wider societal influences. For example, schools can ensure all children have equality of opportunity when it comes to accessing the school's resources, however, the facilities and resources children have access to outside school will vary considerably, depending on the income of the child's parents and the area in which they live. Similarly, if the child goes home to a safe, warm house where those that look after them are not unusually stressed by other life events, they are going to have very different experience to those children who may not have such security at home or whose carers are concerned about money, jobs, unemployment and repossession. Such differences in background will also impact on the child's sense of self, sense of identity and expectations (Dunlop, 2006).

Children who have a range of microsystems to move between grow-up understanding, whether consciously or unconsciously, how to manage themselves in a range of social and cultural situations. They build up a repertoire of behaviours and a bank of knowledge and understanding that can build confidence and self-esteem. They learn that the world is full of different situations but they have a range of experiences they can draw on to help them deal with a new and unfamiliar situation they may find themselves in. The broader the micro-systems available to the child, the greater the child's access to a range of social and cultural experiences and understanding, the higher a child's store of social capital (Dunlop, 2006: 3). For example, a child who is used to travelling out of their immediate home environment, to stay with relatives, for example; or the child who goes to play-group, friends' houses, travels abroad on holiday, does activities outside the home and is encouraged to engage with a range of ideas, will have more social skills at their disposal and will have learnt that new situations can bring exciting possibilities compared to a child who has, for whatever reasons, a more restricted microsystem.

## The notion of family

Both the work of Bowlby and Bronfenbrenner highlight the fundamental impact a child's immediate family has on all aspects of growth and development. This next section explores what is meant by the term 'family', since it is a term that can mean many things, depending on who is using it. Interestingly, in our exploration of why family is important, through looking at Bowlby's theory of the importance of attachment to a child's thriving and flourishing and Bronfrenbrenner's work, both of them state that children having family is important, but neither of them say what a 'family' should 'look like'. This is further illustrated by Featherstone (2004) who states: 'humans have been imagining and re-imagining families throughout recorded history' (Featherstone, 2004: 20). That is to say, many of us have an image of what we think a family is – or should be – having often 'picked up' this image of the family from the popular discourse about families. However, we also know that the reality is that there is no one model for determining what a family is. Families too come in diverse configurations, shapes and sizes.

However, while our experience teaches us that no one family is like another, one of the most enduring notions of what constitutes a family is the discourse surrounding the notion of the 'nuclear family' encouraged in the 1950s. This concept of family portrays a family as being one constituted of a 'male employed head of household, homemaker wife and dependent children in a nuclear arrangement' (Featherstone, 2004: 20; Chambers, 2001; Knowles, 2009). Indeed Chambers (2001) would go further and claim that this portrayal of the family 'reinforces a white, middle-class, patriarchal model … shaped by British imperial power and activated in the colonial context' (Chambers, 2001: 33). However, even the most cursory research will expose this model as not reflecting the family experience of the majority of children and adults. Indeed, research by the Family Policy Studies Centre in 2000 shows that 'one in four children will experience the divorce of their parents by the time they are 16' (Foley et al., 2001: 239), and a similar number of households are supported by a 'lone parent'. Many divorced parents will remarry, forming stepfamilies, however, 'estimates also suggest that at least 50 percent of remarriages that form a stepfamily also end in divorce, and that a quarter of step families break down in the first year'. (Foley et al., 2001: 239)

Families are of central importance to society since they are the means by which societies reproduce themselves. At a very fundamental level a society needs children since it needs them to grow up and become the adults that run the society. Children become the adults that govern society, fill the jobs, generate a country's wealth and continue to ensure economic growth. At a very pragmatic level, a society needs families, in part, because they are one of the mechanisms by which children can be generated. Not only this, but most children are born into families that want them and are prepared to selflessly seek to provide for the needs of the child. Most families also seek to educate and socialize their children to grow up to be the next generation and take on the responsibility of managing society. While this discussion of what families are about may seem to reduce the notion of family to a structure that is there to serve society, it is still worth considering families in this way since society needs families and needs them in all their diversity, and harms both itself and children by pursuing a dominant discourse that suggests the only good family is the family that meets the nuclear family model.

From our exploration of the work of Bowlby and Bronfenbrenner we know that what young children need to thrive are caregivers with whom they can form secure, mutually affectionate bonds. Although in his early work Bowlby saw the child's birthmother as being the ideal person to fulfil this role, the most positive impact of Bowlby's work is in recognizing that what a child needs is not necessarily their birthmother, however desirable a situation that may seem, but a caregiver or caregivers who can provide security and affection. Similarly, we can see from the work of Bronfenbrenner that a child who is growing up in an environment with a range of stimuli and socializing experiences and with caregivers who can mitigate the worst of the negative events that may be happening in society, while enjoying the positive aspects of life society has to offer, will be a thriving child. Therefore, as adults who work with children, we need to have a broad understanding of what family might mean to any one child and to society as a whole.

 Activity

Think about ways in which outstanding schools can celebrate family diversity.

Overall, does the school generate a sense of all families being valued and respected?

When the school sends out letters and information to a child's home, is there an assumption it is the child's mother who is the audience for the letter or information?

Is the information sent home in a language that can be understood at home?

How are children's families encouraged to work in partnership with school to support particular needs a child might have?

Do home corners in KS1 allow children to act out their home lives 'helping them to learn more about how families are different' (Ofsted, 2007: 31)?

Is the personal, social and health education aspect of the curriculum used to best effect to enable children to 'share news about themselves and their families, helping them develop a strong sense of belonging and being valued' (Ofsted, 2007: 24)?

*(Continued)*

*(Continued)*

Do displays, books and other information and resources around the school reflect the diversity of family life both in terms of different cultures and the different ways a family might be constituted?

Does the school actively engage with all aspects of the school's community? Do children have the opportunity to go out into the community? Are community members prominent members of school life?

Are children and their families for whom English is an additional language supported, both to learn English and through information being available in a variety of languages?

Do adults in the school work closely with children's families, listening to what they have to say about individual children and their interests?

In Reception do key workers liaise with the children's families? Are the children's family members 'encouraged to spend time in the setting with their children when they start attending, to build the child's confidence in their new carer' (Ofsted, 2007: 25)?

OfSTED states: 'outstanding providers recognise the fact that parents know their children best … They work hard to draw parents into their child's learning' (Ofsted, 2007: 27).

## Parental responsibility

The law understands the term parental responsibility as 'the bundle of rights and duties relating to a child' (www.family-lawfirm.co.uk/), which derive from a range of family laws that have been passed over a period of time. In this way the law sees parental responsibility as including providing for the material needs of a child, a home, food, clothing and education. In British law a child's mother automatically has parental responsibility. An unmarried father of a child does not automatically have parental responsibility, even where the father may be registered on the child's birth certificate. Therefore, in a family where the child's parents may be living together, but unmarried, it may only be the mother who has parental responsibility. 'Fathers without parental responsibility are able to acquire it through a formal agreement registered with the authorities or through a Court Order' (www.family-lawfirm.co.uk/). Grandparents may have parental responsibility, as may other members of a child's family, depending on the family circumstances and, 'following the Civil Partnership Act 2004 coming into force on the 5th December 2005 same sex partners in a registered Civil Partnership are also able to acquire parental responsibility by formal agreement or Court Order' (www. family-lawfirm.co.uk/). Schools do need to be aware of who has parental responsibility for a child as they too are bound by legislation in terms of who they must contact as the 'parents' of a child. However, while we have briefly explored what the law says about who has parental responsibility for a child, from the child's point of view they may regard their family, that is, the unit of people they go home to, differently. Similarly, the group of people a child regards as their family may vary greatly from child to child and be comprised of a range of those they are related to by birth or bound to by law or through other social relationships.

Children will have families where one adult, who may or may not be a birth parent, may be looking after them. Older siblings may be responsible for the family unit. Families will be comprised of step-parents and possibly step-brothers and sisters, or half-brothers and sisters. Aunts, uncles and grandparents may be integral family members having parental responsibility, morally and financially, if not legally, for children. Children will have parents who are a same sex couple or they may be living in foster families, be a Child in Care or be with an adopted family.

## Step-parents

When an adult becomes a step-parent they do not automatically gain parental responsibility. However, where appropriate, since 2005, it can be applied for. For a step-parent to gain parental responsibility each person with parental responsibility for a child is required to sign the agreement. However, while it is important to be clear where legal responsibility for a child lies, the relationships children will have with those they regard as family will be complex and fluid and vice versa. Step-parenting and being a step-child is by far from being a new family concept. However, before the 1960s and changes to the divorce laws, step-families usually occurred because of a bereavement, where one parent had died and the surviving parent re-married. The rise in the number of children with step-parents and adults who find themselves in the role of step-parent has led to far greater discussion and understanding of how the step-child–parent relationship might develop.

From the step-parent's point of view, it is usually the person they are marrying who is their primary reason for forming the relationship in the first instance. They may already have children of their own or be childless. They will have a range of feelings about becoming a step-parent. However, what research in this area has found is that while there are well embedded role models about being a father or mother to fall back on, this is not so with a step-relationship. It may be necessary to enter the 'step' relationship with a much more open mind about how the relationship will develop and what rules it will be governed by.

The 'big concern' for both the child and the adult entering into a step-relationship can be, is the relationship supposed to mirror a birthparent/child relationship – or is it something different? For a child who has a relationship with their birthparents, although they may spend a majority of their time with one of their parents, often the last thing they want is for a step-parent to become a 'new' mother or father. Indeed, many step-parents do not want that for the relationship either (Waterman, 2003). Children too will feel a range of emotions for the step-parent, from resentment to affection, or they may be torn between loyalty to their birthparent and actually quite liking this new person. 'Research suggests that stepmothers tend to have a more difficult time in their role than stepfathers' (www.family lawfirm.co.uk/). Also, 'many stepfathers take on a lot of responsibility – emotionally, practically and financially – but may feel they have no power and aren't appreciated' (www.family-lawfirm.co.uk/).

 Case studies

Charlotte says: 'my parents divorced when I was two and both remarried quite quickly, so, growing-up I had a step-mother and a step-father. Then I had half-brothers and sisters. As a very young child I hated both step-parents and wanted my birthparents to get back together again. I was particularly horrible to my step-mother who I think I took all my anger out on. We talk about it now (and laugh) and she says she thinks she wasn't very nice to me either – but the funny thing is, I can't remember that at all. I tell my children how awful I was to her and they know her as 'nana' and are appalled that I did those things to their nana.'

'As I got older I began to realize that there were things about these two 'step' people that were actually better than my birthparents and I began to develop a different sort of relationship with them. It's hard to explain, it's not like they are your parents, but you would still go to the ends of the earth for them. My step-father died a few years ago after a long illness. It was really difficult to know how to handle it, there was no guidance for what to do. When he died no one said how sorry they were to me – like they would if he had been my father, it's very hard to explain that sort of relationship to others. I have a friend whose parents divorced and her mum remarried. She got on really well with her step-father, but that marriage broke up too. She missed him dreadfully, but it was really hard for her having a birth dad and then a step-dad, who was, technically no-longer her step-dad. She tries to stay in contact with her 'ex' step-father but he's in another relationship now which makes it even harder.'

## Questions for discussion

Who, for you, have been the most important people in your 'family' throughout your life?
Are you related to these people by birth or marriage?
Or, are they people whom you have met over the years and have become central to your life?
How do we distinguish between people who are our friends and those who are our family?

Charlotte's experience of being step-parented is echoed by Waterman (2003) who writes:

It helps children to have a mother and a stepmother (or birthmother and adoptive mother, foster and biological mother, grandmother and mother) whom they can idealize for different attributes over time (if the loyalty conflict can be outgrown), as in the case of my husband, who reveres his mother for her passion and intensity of feeling and his late stepmother for her integrity and artistic sensibilities; and each of them for their Nicaraguan and Norwegian cooking, respectively. (Waterman, 2003: 99)

Sometimes step-parents can be a huge relief to children. Depending on what their family situation had been before the arrival of a step-parent. Sometimes birthparents who have been through a difficult break-up or divorce have relied on the child to 'parent' them. This can force the child to have to take on responsibilities they are too young for or mean the child is missing out on the parenting they need. A step-parent joining the family can redress this balance and allow the child to hand over some of their responsibilities. 'Thus by maintaining boundaries between the generations, stepparents can provide their stepchildren with a sense that at least one parent is in charge while biological parents are struggling to re-group post-divorce' (Waterman, 2003: 99). While not all step-parenting works out, not all birth-parenting is without its problems too and this is picked up again in Chapter 8. However, what schools do need to be aware of is how the child in the relationship views the relationship. What does the child call their step-parent(s)? When they make Mother's Day cards what do they make for their step-mother?

## Lesbian and gay parenting

A further change in families which it is important to recognize is how, over the past 20 years, a greater awareness of the role of lesbian and gay families in the lives of children has developed. As we have just discussed: 'the past 50 years have seen us remodel the family as step-families and single parenthood has become commonplace' (Hannon, 2009). Similarly:

> this has been accompanied by profound shifts in our views on what good parenting looks like. The rise of gay families is a part of the next chapter of this change, and it should not be provocative to suggest that there might be things to learn from alternative approaches to parenting and kinship. (Hannon, 2009)

Further to this, although discussing parenting by gay or same-sex couples, Tasker (2005) could be discussing family life in all its diversity when she states: 'children of lesbian or gay parents have similar experiences of family life compared with children in heterosexual families' (Tasker, 2005: 224–40). Where 'issues' about family and family life arise is when people seem to be challenged by others having diverse families that conflict with their notion of what families 'should' be like (Tasker, 2005: 224–40).

Throughout our discussion about family diversity, and diverse childhoods, the central theme has been, that for a child to thrive and therefore achieve at school, they need a home where they feel valued and are cared for, both physically and emotionally. It is likely that each child's home will be unique and that this uniqueness will be reflected in the child's identity. Our role, as those seeking to enable children to achieve in their education, is to recognize the strength in the diversity of family life and to work with the child's family, and the child's sense of identity, to allow the child to draw on the support they derive from home to enable them to achieve in their learning.

## Further reading 📖

- Chambers, D. (2001) *Representing the Family*. London: Sage.
- Deater-Deckard, K. (2004) *Parenting Stress*. New Haven, CT: Yale University Press.
- Empson, J. (2004) *Atypical Child Development in Context*. Basingstoke: Palgrave Macmillan.
- Featherstone, B. (2004) *Family Life and Family Support: A Feminist Analysis*. Basingstoke: Palgrave Macmillan.

- Foley, P., Roche, J. and Tucker, S., (2001) *Children in Society: Contemporary Theory, Policy and Practice.* Basingstoke: Palgrave/Open University.

- Mayseless, O. (2002) *Parenting Representations: Theory, Research, and Clinical Implications.* Cambridge: Cambridge University Press.

- Tasker, F. (2005) 'Lesbian Mothers, Gay Fathers, and Their Children: A Review', *Journal of Developmental & Behavioral Pediatrics 26*(3): 224–40.

## Useful websites

- Becoming a step parent: http://www.bbc.co.uk/health/physical_health/family/stepfamilies/step_becoming.shtml

  o Advice and support for step-families

- Growing kids: http://www.growingkids.co.uk/GayLesbianParents.html

  o Advice and information for families with gay and lesbian parents

# Ethnicity, Whiteness and Identity

## Vini Lander

> **This chapter explores:**
> - the meaning and importance of the term ethnicity;
> - how ethnicity and achievement are linked;
> - the notion of whiteness which is emerging as a concept in the literature on race and education in England;
> - how the concepts discussed in the chapter enable practitioners to reflect on and evaluate their own position with regard to these discussions and identify how their practice can be changed to accommodate their new understanding for the greater benefit of children, young people, their families and communities.

Issues related to race, ethnicity and identity and how these aspects affect our own positionality (Bell, in Taylor et al., 2009) are complex and often require some reflection. They may also require revisiting. The concept of 'positionality' is used to help us explore where we believe ourselves to be 'positioned' in terms of discussions about race, ethnicity and whiteness. That is to say, our own ethnicity, whether we describe ourselves as being Black, White or mixed-race will, to a certain extent, determine how we engage with the debate about these concepts and where we are 'positioned' by our cultural and life experiences in the discussion. As professionals working to help all children enjoy and achieve we have a legal, and many would argue, a moral duty to be informed about issues related to race and ethnicity and to know how to construct arguments to oppose negative attitudes or positions towards and about race – attitudes and positions which we may come across socially and in schools. Being critical and questioning is part of developing as a professional across all aspects of the work we do in schools, and for the reasons we have already explored, for our work in the field of equality, diversity and achievement it is important that we become conversant with the debates about race, ethnicity and multiculturalism. In fact it is important that we develop a multicultural literacy, regardless of the area we live in within our diverse society. Understanding these debates not only enables us to define our own position but also enables us to better understand how to promote equality of opportunity for all children. This, in turn, enables them to succeed within the education system, to be healthy, safe, enjoy and achieve, to make a positive contribution and to achieve economic well-being (DfES, 2004).

## What is ethnicity? Why is it important?

It is important to acknowledge that we all have ethnicity. The term 'ethnicity' or 'ethnic' can seem only to relate to images of Asian, African or African-Caribbean people. The term seems inextricably associated with people of colour. Yet on the 'ethnic monitoring forms' we fill out for applications for jobs or a university place many ethnicities are listed, not only those associated with skin colour. Ethnicity is an interesting and contested concept because it encompasses a number of dimensions which serve to contribute to the whole notion of what is meant by ethnicity. These components are aspects such as history, nationality, language and religion. So English, Irish, Scottish, Welsh, Muslim, Sikh and Cypriot are ethnicities which people could define themselves by. In essence, ethnicity encompasses common elements which people use to differentiate themselves into a group. Smith (2009) notes that the origin of the word ethnic comes from the Latin *ethnicus* and he goes on to highlight that in ecclesiastical Latin it means 'heathen'. This is very interesting because the term was used to identify people who were not Christian or Jewish and therefore the 'other'. 'Other' carried with it implications of being an 'outsider', being the 'lesser', the 'lower' and conversely this implies the 'higher' and the suggestion that there are those that are 'better'. In the use of the term there is an inherent assumption of a hierarchy which still permeates thinking and attitudes to ethnicity today. The ethnicities delineated below are the categories on one form found on the internet. The ethnicities that the form includes and fails to list, plus the order in which the ethnicities are listed, can be said to convey many messages, however unwittingly, about how ethnicities are ranked and valued. If you are Chinese, or from an Arab background how do you feel about this form? If you are mixed-race which category would you choose to say you belong to? What might the term 'other' on the form convey?

Ethnic monitoring categories

1 White

   a British
   b Irish
   c Other

2 Mixed

   a White and Black Caribbean
   b White and Black African
   c White and Asian

3 Asian or Asian British

   a Indian
   b Pakistani
   c Bangladeshi

4 Black or Black British

   a Caribbean
   b African

5 Other ethnic group

 ## Case study

Saleema is a student teacher in year 1 of an undergraduate degree. She does not know which box to tick because her parents came to this country when they were young and she was born in Britain and feels she is British, but with a Pakistani Muslim cultural heritage. She feels she has more affinity with Britain than Pakistan, although she does have relatives she visits there. She feels she is a Muslim in terms of her identity but there isn't a box that defines her identity which she feels is British Muslim. She feels more comfortable with this identity rather than 'Asian British' or 'Pakistani'.

 ## Questions for discussion

Reflecting back to the discussions about identity in Chapter 2, why is it important for Saleema – or anyone – to be able to indicate as accurately as possible what they see as their ethnic identity on such forms?

How does conducting ethnic monitoring in this way add to society's understanding about ethnicity and whiteness?

Just as Saleema is unsure how the form reflects her identity and ethnicity, if you are White British you may feel that you want to identify yourself as white English, or Welsh as that conveys your identity more accurately. If you are from a mixed-heritage background you may struggle even more with the 'given' categories that often are pre-selected for forms like this. In this way, we can begin to understand the contested nature of ethnicity as a defining concept. However, these are important discussions to continue to have since, as a diverse society, we need a way in which we can monitor our progress in promoting equality of opportunity and children's achievement in education as well as our success in meeting our legal obligations with respect to the Race Relations Amendment Act 2000.

## Race, racism and institutional racism – what does it matter?

There is no doubt that race is a contested term, a term whose meaning has no agreed definition, this is why it is shown in inverted commas in most texts. Many would argue that there is no such thing as different races but just one race – the human race. It is true that our genetic make-up is essentially the same, with only a small proportion that is different, although some scientists would contest this too. Indeed we are more the same than different. However, if we are more same than different then why do we make a big issue of race or ethnicity? The answer partly lies in the fact that race is a social construct (Garner, 2010). That is, a construction designed by humans. The notion of 'race' is not just limited to a signifier of physical differences, it has in the past been extended to attribute characteristics, qualities and attributes given to different peoples. This was the case during the slave trade when the black slaves were not even considered to be humans but regarded as property (Harris, 1993). In this way many myths were perpetuated which remain in the social psyche today. Ryde (2009: 35) notes, 'Today's racism is hard-wired into our consciousness from the prejudices of the past'. This is the result of the powerful exerting control and domination over the less powerful and creating stories and myths to retain their power and maintain their oppression.

Indeed there are still many myths that prevail which are perpetuated by some parts of the popular press such as in headlines which herald that we are being *overrun* by immigrants, asylum seekers and refugees. When people are asked to estimate the percentage of Black and Minority Ethnic (BME) people their responses vary from 30% to 10%. The last census in 2001 showed that the BME population was

7.9%, with 45% of the total BME population living in London (Office for National Statistics, n.d.). However, the actual situation with regard to the statistics can be overshadowed by the impression created by some of the media, an impression which can often generate ill feeling, suspicion, prejudice or racism against certain groups.

Those working in education and the wider schools' workforce can feel uncomfortable with discussions about race, ethnicity or racism, particularly the last word. This discomfort can arise depending on people's experience, or lack of experience. For example, those who have lived in culturally homogenous areas may have no experience of having witnessed acts of overt racism, acts which can range from low-level name calling to acts of violence. They may not yet have had the opportunity to think through some of the issues around racism, they may have never met people from minority ethnic backgrounds, or had the opportunity yet to work with children from minority ethnic backgrounds or with those for whom English is an additional language (EAL) and, therefore may not yet have the language or concepts to talk about the issues.

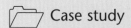 Case study

Kulwant is 13 years old now and this is an account about his primary schooling. He was born in England. Since starting school he has made some friends but not a best friend. At playtimes he would wander about the playground to see if someone would play with him. Sometimes the other children would let him play but most times they didn't. There were not very many BME children in the school. He felt that maybe it was because he was different that they didn't play with him. There were about four people who were from BME backgrounds. There was Michael, he was Black and his mum and dad came from Nigeria; then there was Rashida, she was Muslim and she was in Year 6 and the other child who was Chinese was called Roy. They all spoke English very well. Kulwant always thought that they didn't want to play with him because he was a Sikh boy, he has long hair which is coiled into a top-knot under his patka (a cloth which covers the head and hair). Some children called him 'bobble-head'. He would get really angry and hurt by this. He told his mum and she told him to tell his teacher first. So he did. Mrs Clarke said 'Don't worry about it my dear. Sticks and stones … you know' (but Kulwant wasn't sure what she meant); 'you are so much better than they are anyway. Take no notice'. Well that was useful. He just thought she was unhelpful and he had

*(Continued)*

*(Continued)*

thought she was there to help him. She didn't understand and she didn't seem to care. He knew what they were saying was racist, but he knew he couldn't do anything about it. If he told his mum again she would come to the school and make a fuss and he felt then the teachers and the children wouldn't like him and so he really would have no friends then.

Then suddenly the teachers realized what it was all about but it was too late. By then Kulwant was in the last few weeks of Year 6. He felt the children who were being hurtful had got away with it and that teachers did nothing. There was one boy in particular who had always bothered Kulwant and called him names like 'smelly Paki', and 'Taliban', and he pushed him about. Kulwant didn't do anything to him for fear of getting into trouble. One day as he played football in the playground this lad came up behind Kulwant and gave him such a big push and thump that Kulwant fell over and was knocked out by the fall. The next thing Kulwant was aware of was that he was in an ambulance going to hospital and his Year 6 teacher was with him. Following this event his mum went to see the headteacher, who actually apologized for what had happened and said, 'We appear to have failed Kulwant'. Kulwant felt too right they did!

 Questions for discussion

As a reflective practitioner what clues would have alerted you that there were issues of racism that were affecting Kulwant's well-being? Thinking through this case study, how does it help explore how racism is different from other sorts of name calling associated with being fat or wearing glasses, for example?

Your response to Kulwant's story will depend on a number of factors, including: your experience of dealing with such situations, the training you have had to deal with issues like this, whether you have had racism directed at you – or whether you have said something like Kulwant's teacher did, perhaps because you did not know what else to do. Schools, like other public institutions, are compelled to meet the duty set out in the Race Relations Amendment Act 2000 and have a duty to promote community cohesion (DCSF, 2007a).

Racism as defined by Macpherson (1999) is 'conduct or words or practices which advantage or disadvantage people because of their colour, culture or ethnic origin'. (www.archive.official-documents. co.uk/document/cm42/4262/sli-00.htm)

**Activity**

Try reflecting on the following.
In what ways can racism:

- advantage a person?
- disadvantage a person?

When you hear the word racism what picture springs into your mind?

Racism is no longer an issue confined to Black–White issues. It is more accurate to refer to 'racisms' because there are a range of exclusionary responses to difference which result in disadvantage or detrimental outcomes. The term includes racism, as defined above, xenophobia and anti-Semitism. The term racisms acknowledges that factors other than skin colour or culture can engender hatred, discrimination, exclusion and disadvantage (Parekh, 2000). This has been the case since 9/11 which generated hatred, against Muslims which is referred to as islamophobia (Garner, 2010; Gillborn, 2009). Acts of racism or racist attitudes are premised on the superiority of one culture, or religion, or way of life. This creates a hierarchy of acceptability or tolerance and leads to the devaluing of the 'other' and the privileging of a mainstream culture which is cast as more acceptable or the norm which is used to judge other cultures by. The more the culture deviates from the norm, which in Britain is thought to be White middle class and Christian the more likely you are to be excluded from society (see Chapter 7 on Gypsy, Roma and Travellers).

## Institutional racism

Whilst you may be shocked by Kulwant's story because it outlines acts of overt racism, such racism can still occur across all sectors and institutions in British society. However, Richardson (2004: 19) distinguishes between overt and institutional racism; the former as the racism that kills and the latter as racism that discriminates. Previously, the latter form of racism was described as 'passive' racism. However, there is nothing passive about institutional racism. Institutional racism exists as a result of people deciding to do nothing about the inequity which they see or are aware of around them. It does not affect them so they do nothing. They are then as complicit in racism as those involved in any violent racist act. In reading Kulwant's story many readers would be left questioning the inaction of the teachers in his school and the school's position, particularly in the light of national legislation. But the inactions of the school can be classified as institutional racism. It is hard to recognize and acknowledge institutional racism. It is a pervasive form of racism which as a society we still seem to have failed to address. This may be for a number of reasons. Institutional racism is embedded in everyday practices of institutions and the people that implement the processes and practices of that institution. This does not mean that the individuals are themselves racists.

 Case study

Look at the extracts below taken from The Stephen Lawrence Inquiry (Macpherson, 1999). (Note that the abbreviation MPS stands for the Metropolitan Police Service.)

1.11 Stephen Lawrence's murder was simply and solely and unequivocally motivated by racism. It was the deepest tragedy for his family. It was an affront to society, and especially to the local black community in Greenwich.

2.5 The Inquest jury returned a unanimous verdict after a full hearing in 1997, that 'Stephen Lawrence was unlawfully killed in a completely unprovoked racist attack by five white youths'.

2.10 There is no doubt whatsoever but that the first MPS investigation was palpably flawed and deserves severe criticism. Nobody listening to the evidence could reach any other conclusion. This is now plainly accepted by the MPS. Otherwise the abject apologies offered to Mr & Mrs Lawrence would be meaningless.

2.11 The underlying causes of that failure are more troublesome and potentially more sinister. The impact of incompetence and racism, and the aura of corruption or collusion have been the subject of much evidence and debate.

5.31 Yet at the end of the day we are satisfied that the lack of respect and sensitivity in handling him must reflect unwitting and collective racism particularly in those who dealt with him both at the scene of the murder and at the hospital ... was the victim of racist stereotyping.

 Questions for discussion

What does the Macpherson Inquiry state motivated Stephen's killing?
What conclusions does the Macpherson inquiry draw from the MPS's apology to Stephen's parents?
What attitudes and behaviour prevalent in the MPS did the Inquiry find 'flawed' in the investigation into Stephen's death?
What do you think Macpherson means when he uses the terms unwitting and collective racism?

The term institutional racism came to public attention through the Macpherson Inquiry in 1999 which was set up to examine the circumstances which led to the inability of the Metropolitan Police to apprehend the murderers of the Black teenager, Stephen Lawrence. The Macpherson Report (1999) defined institutional racism as:

> The collective failure of an organisation to provide an appropriate and professional service to people because of their colour, culture, or ethnic origin. It can be seen or detected in processes, attitudes and behaviour which amount to discrimination through unwitting prejudice, ignorance, thoughtlessness and racist stereotyping which disadvantage minority ethnic people. It persists because of the failure of the organisation openly and adequately to recognise and address its existence and causes by policy, example and leadership. Without recognition and action to eliminate such racism it can prevail as part of the ethos or culture of the organisation. It is a corrosive disease. (Macpherson, 1999: Paragraph 6.34)

Where people dispute the idea of institutional racism, it can be because they do not understand or have a limited understanding about how power and oppression operate. Nonetheless, it can also betray the power or superior position that is conveyed by the speaker. However, institutional racism is difficult to identify. Firstly, institutional racism is not apparent in overtly racist language or actions; the evidence of its operation is evident in statistics such as in recruitment, retention, progression and achievement of BME people or employees within an institution. Secondly, because it is 'hidden' or rather unapparent to some people it can be easily denied and therefore nothing is done to advance an institution beyond its discriminatory practices and unequal outcomes. It must be noted that any form of racism is premised on the notion of superiority, and is exerted from a position of power which allows the individual or institution to exercise their power through action or inaction which is discriminatory. The continued presence of institutional, hidden, or passive racism is described beautifully through the metaphor of a moving walkway by Beverly Tatum (1999).

> I sometimes visualize the ongoing cycle of racism as a moving walkway at the airport. Active racist behaviour is equivalent to walking fast on the conveyor belt. The person engaged in active racist behaviour has identified with the ideology of White supremacy and is moving with it. Passive racist behaviour is equivalent to standing still on the walkway. No overt effort is being made, but the conveyor belt moves the bystanders along to the same destination as those who are actively walking. Some of the bystanders may feel the motion of the conveyor belt, see the active racists ahead of them, and choose to turn around, unwilling to go to the same destination as the White supremacists. But unless they are walking actively in the opposite direction at a speed faster than the conveyor belt – unless they are actively antiracist – they'll find themselves carried along with the others. (Tatum, 1999: 11–12)

## Whiteness – what is it? How can *that* be important?

Some of the most common responses in discussions about race, ethnicity, racism and diversity are usually in the following vain 'Everyone is the same. I don't see colour. You are an individual to me'. If these phrases are said by someone White, it is often as a way of diverting or rendering the debate null and void. And some would see this as an appropriate liberal position to take, however, such statements can also be an expression of power and privilege. Not seeing my colour, which is a strong part of my identity (indeed other people have drawn attention to it) is a way of denying my identity. Worse still, by using such terms I am rendered invisible or being made 'White by proxy' as it is termed by Jones (1999). Using such statements has the power to negate my identity and provide me with a cloak of whiteness. And when thought through in this way one recognizes the ridiculousness of such statements. This neutral 'colour blind' position can not only deny BME people their identity but it can also deny them their experience of racism through a privileged, possibly myopic, perspective which seeks, but fails, to address issues of race and racism as realities in my world and that of other BME people.

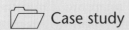 Case study

> Jyoti is a newly qualified teacher in her first job in a suburban school in a southern county in England. She hears a conversation in the staffroom between two colleagues about immigration and they use the term 'paki'. They go on to to discuss that they saw nothing wrong with the term nigger because in the 1950s there were brown stockings called 'nigger brown' and someone's granny at the time owned a dog called Nigger because he was all black. Jyoti becomes quite uncomfortable and clears her throat to say something but one of her colleagues interjects, 'Oh we didn't mean you dear. You're different!'
>
> Jyoti is left feeling hurt, confused and flabbergasted. She asks herself 'How am I different? Why am I different?'

 Questions for discussion

> What would you do if you were Jyoti? Would you complain? Would you want to 'rock the boat' in your first job?

This incident exemplifies the notion of whiteness and white privilege. King (2004: 73) refers to a form of racism which she calls 'dysconscious' racism described as an 'uncritical habit of mind (including perceptions, attitudes, assumptions and beliefs) that justifies inequity by accepting the existing order of things as given'. By assigning this way of being as 'dysconscious' King is not implying that the person is unconscious of what is happening around them but that they demonstrate impaired consciousness, accepting the status quo in which racial inequity is unchallenged, as are the stereotypes, myths and beliefs that perpetuate it. Alongside this there is an implicit acceptance of the advantages which privilege White people and disadvantage others. It could be argued that there are similarities between institutional racism and so-called passive racism. But this notion of dysconscious racism does not let the majority of the population who are inactive with respect to issues of racial inequality 'off the hook'. They cannot claim not to know or to be conscious of it. The next section describes how this dysconscious racism is embedded in the notion of whiteness.

## Whiteness

Marx (2006: 45) has described defining whiteness as an exercise in 'illuminating the invisible'. She notes that whiteness is not applicable to White people *per se* but it is a notion which is embedded in the 'normal' everyday fabric of society, and in this way whiteness has become normalized. It is a function of 'White culture, interests, language, etc.' (Marx, 2006: 45). Zeus Leonardo (2002: 31) presents the distinction concisely: '"Whiteness" is a racial discourse, whereas the category "white people" represents a socially constructed identity, usually based on skin colour'.

In Critical Race Theory (CRT) 'whiteness' is a discourse which has become established through the process of oppression and domination. It is a negative discourse of White talk (McIntyre, 1997: 45), neutrality, colour-blindness and racism. Whiteness pervades institutions to replicate the power and privilege associated with it. It is considered as the 'norm', the status quo and seen as a 'raceless' state. As argued earlier, race and ethnicity are attributes possessed by the 'other'. Many White people may not think of themselves as racialized beings but as the 'norm', particularly where the dominant White culture in a society has become what Hinman (2003) terms uncritically accepted 'as the way things are' (Hinman, 2003: 339). In societies where a particular viewpoint prevails, those that are part of the dominant culture and have that 'normal' view cannot 'experience themselves as outsiders in their own culture. Indeed, they see no difference between their culture and culture' (Hinman, 2003: 339). Therefore, where whiteness is the dominant cultural view White is considered neutral, normal, invisible and often impartial and, in such societies, it may be only those who are other who 'feel the difference' (Hinman, 2003: 339). That is to say, even in situations where members of the dominant culture do experience discrimination their reaction can still be 'to wonder what is wrong with those discriminating against them' (Hinman, 2003: 339), rather than to critically examine the whole notion of how power and discrimination can operate in a society. So we can see how if we apply Marx's (2006) thinking about whiteness to Jyoti's case study, the other teachers in Jyoti's staff room tried to 'normalize' Jyoti to make her fit in to their view of how the world should be. They tried to make Jyoti 'acceptable' by making her White-by-proxy rather than accepting Jyoti as *herself* and Black. Such experiences as Jyoti's can be for BME people an everyday present fact of their lives and one which affects the course of their journey through the day and through their lives (Hinman, 2003; Marx, 2006).

To pursue these ideas further, let us consider the work of McIntosh (1990). In her writing McIntosh (1990) enumerates 46 taken-for-granted privileges she enjoys as a White person merely as a result of her being white. Similarly, echoing the work of Hinman (2003) above, Ryde (2009) notes that White people think race is a problem that BME people have. In exploring this idea, as a 'helping professional' she discusses how she needs to understand her own position as a White person as part of helping others as a counsellor. In her journey to understand whiteness she acknowledges how the discussion about whiteness, its neutrality, the associated privilege and its inherent racism made her feel shame and guilt. Gaine (2001) has also chronicled similar reactions experienced by White student teachers undertaking race equality training. In this instance they too stated that exploring these concepts challenged them and made them feel guilty and that it hurt – it was painful to have to consider these ideas. These feelings were acknowledged and the students continued to work with the training into their careers as teachers. In undertaking discussion of these notions Gaine (2001) claims that 'if it's not hurting it's not working'. Similarly, Solomon et al. (2005) describe, in their work, how discussions about McIntosh's paper on White privilege elicited negative responses from student teachers who proceeded to deny the existence of such privilege. However, this discourse of denial will usually be part of the discussion whenever whiteness and its associated concepts are explored.

## Critical Race Theory (CRT)

This is a theory which has been devised by Black African-Americans in the USA in response to the persistence of racism in society and its institutions (Delgado and Stefancic, 2001). The theory originates within USA legal studies and states that society is inherently racist and that liberal, neutral and colour-blind approaches are ineffective and that most often they form the foundations of White responses to issues of race. The approach places racism and Black people's experiences at the centre and seeks to examine how racism systematically operates to disadvantage people of colour. It is a response to the ineffectiveness of other approaches such as multiculturalism and race legislation in the USA. In England it is an emerging theory which researchers and scholars are just beginning to explore in terms of its applicability to the UK context.

Gillborn (2008), in applying CRT to the British context, asserts that the systematic disadvantaging of Black pupils within education is not a mere accident or coincidence. He points out that education is an arena in which racism operates through policies designed by policy-makers who are oblivious to the effect their policies will have on BME pupils, particularly Black pupils, because the policy-makers operate within a liberal White milieu and in exercising privilege associated with whiteness they are totally oblivious to the racialized outcomes that their policies may have on Black children in school. Gillborn (2009) asserts that whilst this neglect cannot be deemed to be a political conspiracy, it can however be cast as a conspiracy in legal terms. A conspiracy in law is defined as concerted actions which advantage particular groups and within British education this is largely White middle-class children. But the conspiracy of policy-makers systematically disadvantages Black children (Gillborn, 2009). He cites many examples of this which are discussed later.

The Department for Education, or the Department for Education and Skills as it was in 2006, conducted a Priority Review in 2005–6 to explore the reasons why, of the children excluded from schools, a disproportionately high number of them were Black pupils.

The report noted that, in particular, Black Caribbean pupils were three times more likely to be excluded than White pupils (DfES, 2006b). It highlighted in-school factors such as institutional racism and the perceptions teachers held of Black pupils, and out-of-school

**Table 4.1** Percentage of the maintained school population with a fixed period exclusion in 2003/2004 (DfES, 2006)

| Ethnicity | Percentage exclusion |
| --- | --- |
| White British | 4.95 |
| White and Black Caribbean | 9.65 |
| White and Black African | 5.63 |
| Black Caribbean | 9.61 |
| Any other Black background | 9.79 |

factors such as the demands on Black males to perform their masculinity in certain stereotypical ways that may contribute to the high exclusion of male Black pupils from school. It indicated that the stereotypes of Black males which prevailed amongst teachers and institutional racism were key factors in the high exclusion statistics. The report concluded that in a climate of the Every Child Matters agenda:

> Left to its own devices, the system will conclude that Every Child Matters, but that Black children's failure and social exclusion is to be expected – that they matter a little bit less. Personalisation could empower Black pupils to fulfil their true potential, but not whilst teachers' view of the person is conditioned by subconscious prejudice. (DfES, 2006b: 16)

## Education, ethnicity and achievement

In 2003, the DfES published a report entitled *Aiming High: Raising the Achievement of Minority Ethnic Pupils*, it noted that 30% of Black Caribbean pupils gained five or more GCSEs graded A*–C compared to 40% for Pakistani pupils; 45% for Bangladeshi pupils; 50% for White pupils; 65% for Indian pupils and 73% for Chinese pupils. This persistent underachievement of Black pupils has been documented for the last 30 years. Why is it that Black students are the least successful group? What factors contribute to their underachievement?

Gillborn (2008) notes that the underachievement starts well before Black students undertake their GCSE exams. He charts the low percentage (10.5%) of Black boys and girls (14.5%) in top sets for English and mathematics; how the baseline assessment at age five has resulted from Black pupils outperforming their counterparts at age five but as they proceed through schooling this achievement falls away. It may be appropriate to ask why some groups perform better than Black pupils. This may be due to other factors such as gender and social class. Gillborn (2008) refers to them as the model minorities, Chinese and Indian groups which are held up as achieving well within the education system and therefore 'proof' that racism is not the causal factor for the underachievement of Black groups. But the converse is true because we can also explore the possible operation of power and whiteness in this situation too. That is to say, there exist stereotypical ideas of Indian and Chinese pupils and their families as hard workers and these stereotypes can also operate to affect how mainly White teachers treat these groups of pupils; however, in this instance operating with the stereotype actually enables educational achievement (Gillborn, 2009).

In addition, Gillborn (2008) notes that the change from the baseline assessment to the assessment of pupils using the Foundation Stage Profile has shown that at age five Black children have now become the lowest rated group in terms of achievement in the Early Years. There are many complex factors which affect pupil achievement, such as gender and social class, both of which will be explored further in later chapters. However, taking all factors into account, the research, over a number of years, has shown that, in particular, there is a persistent failure in schools' ability to raise the achievement rate of Black boys. Gillborn (2008) asserts that this ongoing underachievement is due to the lack of awareness on the part of policy-makers regarding the effects particular policies will have on BME groups. Gilborn notes that these policies fail because they do not take race into account. They are not race conscious or, possibly, as King (2004) would put it, policy suffers from persistent dysconcious racism. That the needs of a particular group of children and young people is overlooked by aspects of educational policy might, at best, be deemed a form of neglect. At worst it might also be shown to be the result of a possible further example of institutional racism. Institutional racism which, again, if not addressed will continue to adversely affect the life chances and the opportunities of a particular group of children and young people in our schools.

 Activity

> This chapter began with suggesting that in all aspects of our lives we are positioned by our own ethnicity, cultural heritage and life experience with regard to ethnicity and whiteness. Having now read the chapter, consider the following questions:
>
> Are the ideas in the chapter ones that you are quite familiar with? If this is the case, consider a scenario where you have been asked to explain the concepts discussed in this chapter to colleagues in a school situation. Perhaps colleagues who have not thought about some of these ideas before. How might you begin to discuss them in a professional situation?
>
> Did the material in the chapter engage you in thinking about things that you had not come across before? If this is the case, can you identify what particularly was new to you? Has the chapter made you think differently about ethnicity and whiteness? If it has, can you reflect on what about your thinking has changed?

## Further reading

- Bonnett, A. (2000) *White Identities*. Harlow: Pearson.

- Gaine, C. (2005) *We're All White Thanks: The Persisting Myth about 'White' Schools*. Stoke-on-Trent: Trentham.

- Lawrence, D. (2006) *And Still I Rise: Seeking Justice for Stephen*. London: Faber and Faber.

- Leonardo, Z. (2005) *Critical Pedagogy and Race*. Malden, MA: Blackwell.

- Richardson, B. (2005) *Tell It Like It Is: How our Schools Fail Black Children*. London: Bookmark; Stoke-on-Trent: Trentham.

- Richardson, R. (1990) *Daring to be a Teacher*. Stoke-on-Trent: Trentham.

## Useful websites

- Britkid: www.britkid.org

  o A website about race, racism and life – as seen through the eyes of children

- Multiverse: www.multiverse.ac.uk

  o A website for teacher educators and student teachers addressing the educational achievement of pupils from diverse backgrounds

- Runnymede Trust: www.runnymedetrust.org

  o Runnymede is the UK's leading independent race equality think tank. They generate intelligence for a multi-ethnic Britain through research, network building, leading debate, and policy engagement

- Training and Development Agency for schools: www.tda.gov.uk

  o The national agency and recognized sector body responsible for the training and development of the school workforce

# 5

# Class, Equality and Achievement

## Gianna Knowles

> **This chapter explores:**
>
> - How the concept of class is part of the diversity, equality and achievement in education debate;
> - What is meant by class;
> - The link between class and poverty;
> - An exploration of what is meant by the term 'social capital' and how it is linked to class, diversity, equality and achievement.

Class and its impact on achievement is as complex an area of diversity as any we have discussed so far. One of the fundamental determiners of what is meant by class and to what class someone can be described as belonging to is inextricably, although not exclusively, linked to money. In particular, the occupation and earnings of an individual do, in strictly economic terms, determine the class to which they belong. Why this is so is discussed below. Not only does how much a person earns determine their class, but the earnings of a child's family and the class which the family can be described as belonging to, do still have a direct impact on children's likely educational achievement.

## Class, diversity, equality and achievement

In 2010 the Centre for Analysis of Social Exclusion published a report entitled *An Anatomy of Economic Inequality in the UK – Summary Report of the National Equality Panel*. It states:

The evidence we examine confirms that social background really matters. There are significant differences in 'school readiness' before and when children reach school by parental income and mother's education ... every extra £100 per month in income when children were small was associated with a difference equivalent to a month's development. Rather than being fixed at birth, these differences widen through childhood. (Centre for Analysis of Social Exclusion, 2010: 22)

There is an increasing body of research that supports the notion that children from low-income families achieve less well in school than children from more affluent backgrounds. For example, Mongon and Chapman (2008) discuss 'the depth and persistence of underachievement amongst pupils who come from low income families' (Mongon and Chapman, 2008: 4); Smith (2005) in *Analysing Underachievement in Schools* makes the link between low-income being a contributing factor of underachievement; and in 2008 Ofsted noted research showing 'the close association between poverty and low educational achievement, with pupils from low-income backgrounds continuing to perform less well than more advantaged pupils' (Ofsted, 2008c: 4).

One of the other factors about class that make it important to consider when discussing diversity, equality and achievement is that, while individuals can be deemed as belonging to specific groups because of their gender or ethnicity and we can explore what that might mean for them in terms of need, class is something that applies across gender and ethnicity. Whatever our gender or ethnicity we will be linked to others of different genders and ethnicities by our class. This cross-sectionality can act for some as an enabler in terms of achievement and for others compounds the barriers that can impact on their lack of achievement.

## Case study

Sam is White British and is seven, his friend Ali is of Bangladeshi heritage and his other friend Carl is of African-Caribbean heritage. Sam and Carl both have free school meals as their parents do work, in local supermarkets and take-away restaurants, but they work part time and to achieve a basic standard of living have their income supplemented by benefits. Ali's dad is a maths teacher at a local secondary school. Their teacher says both Sam and Carl are underachieving at the moment, they started school with achievement levels below the national average for five year olds and have not yet 'caught-up'. Ali however, is described as 'a star' especially in mathematics and is likely to do really well by the end of Key Stage 1.

**Questions for discussion**

Do you think socio-economic factors might be contributing to Sam and Carl's underachievement?
What might that mean? How could that happen?
In the same way, could Ali's background contribute in any way to his level of achievement? What might be happening for Ali that is not present in Sam and Carl's life?
The next section might help you with exploring this case study and these questions more critically.

The achievement – or lack of achievement – of the children in this case study is compounded by class and in Carl's case, possibly his ethnicity too. This is a picture of achievement reflected nationally and one also noted by the report: *An Anatomy of Economic Inequality in the UK:*

> In the main data available on performance at school, the best available indicator of socio-economic background is whether children receive Free School Meals. By age 16, half of boys receiving Free School Meals have results in the bottom quarter in England (and in the bottom fifth in Wales). However, it is boys on Free School Meals from certain ethnic backgrounds that slip back through secondary school … By 16 White British, Black Caribbean and mixed White and Black Caribbean boys receiving Free School Meals have the lowest average assessment of any group identified by gender, ethnicity and Free School Meals status, apart from Gypsy and Traveller children. (Centre for Analysis of Social Exclusion, 2010: 23)

This report is only the most recent in a number of research projects that have also found that there is a gap in attainment between classes and linked to class and ethnicity. In 2000 Gillborn and Mirza reported very similar findings to that of the Centre for Analysis of Social Exclusion. However, before we pursue our exploration of the link between class and achievement and discuss the part those who work in education and their values, attitudes and beliefs may play in this issue, let us first be clear about what we mean by class.

## What do we mean by class?

Our current use of the term class and the sub-groups within that, for example the notion of working class middle class, derive from the work of social and political writers and philosophers from the eighteenth century onwards. One of the most influential figures in terms of our understanding of class from this time is the historical and political philosopher Karl Marx (1818–1883). Marx was concerned to explain the sociological and political effects on the population occasioned by Britain's seemingly rapid change from a largely agricultural country to an industrialized one. Britain's rapid industrialization saw the movements of huge numbers of people from farming the land to working in factories and other manufacturing processes. The change also brought with it what are now the infamous slum conditions that many of these economic migrants from the country found themselves living in. Not only this, but many endured appalling working conditions and wages, while the use of child labour was widespread. Marx explored this divide between those who were reaping considerable economic benefit from industrialization and those who were living in poverty. In very general terms he described people as being in one of two groups, or what we might now call classes. Those who were, in his terms, the owners of the 'means of production', who actually owned the factories that produced the goods and therefore pocketed the profits he saw as being in a higher class. The workers, who were far removed from being owners of 'the means of production' and were at the mercy of the factory owners to hire and fire as benefited them, he described in terms that we would now understand as being working class (Wheen, 2000).

In strict terms, those we would now see as being middle class are not necessarily Marx's factory owners, but they are those who are closer to the means of production than the workers. The middle class are the professionals who might hold executive positions in the factories, they may be shareholders in businesses and they will serve as the allied professionals – the lawyers, accountants and bank managers whose services the owners of the means of production would need to support their industries.

In modern terms, the notion of working class and middle class is still linked to the employment people are engaged in, although rather than class the term 'socio-economic classification' is sometimes used. This is the term used by the Office for National Statistics who in ascribing a socio-economic classification to someone use the *Standard Occupational Classification 2000* (Office for National Statistics, 2009). The classification makes a judgement about an occupation based on two criteria: the type of work someone undertakes – the 'job' – and the personal levels of ability and understanding needed to do that job, known as skills (Office for National Statistics, 2009). The more demanding, particularly in intellectual terms the knowledge, understanding and skills needed for the job, the higher the classification of the job. Not only this, but the more demanding the job is in terms of these intellectual skills, the greater the economic benefits to those in those jobs. Simply put, the greater your skills, particularly intellectual skills, the higher your salary. There are nine major categories in the classification, each of which have sub-groups (Office for National Statistics, 2009). The classification of occupations used by the government and drawn up by the Office for National Statistics is the baseline for 'ranking' individuals by occupation. The ranking of the classifications from the Office for National Statistics (2009) is shown in Table 5.1.

With regards to this classification, what is usually seen as the defining feature between which of the occupations listed in Table 5.1 are working class and which are middle class is the level to which someone has to be educated to be employed in that post. That is, those jobs for which you are required to have a degree are deemed to be middle class and those for which you may need no qualifications, or perhaps training, but not to degree level, are working class (Benson, 2003: 12).

**Table 5.1**

| Classification of occupation in rank order | Occupation | Example |
| --- | --- | --- |
| 1 | Managers and senior officials | Heads and executive managers of private and public companies, banks, local government, business, NHS, rail companies, airlines, police officers (inspectors and above) |
| 2 | Professional occupations | Doctors, lawyers, teachers, science and engineering professionals |
| 3 | Associate professional and technical occupations | Laboratory technicians, nurses, midwives, paramedics, speech and language therapists, youth workers, police officers (sergeant and below) |
| 4 | Administrative and secretarial occupations | Filing and other records assistants/clerks, library assistants/clerks, school secretaries |
| 5 | Skilled trades occupations | Plumbers, electricians, brick layers |
| 6 | Personal service occupations | Hairdressers, nursery nurses, childminders, educational assistants |
| 7 | Sales and customer service occupations | Shop workers, call centre operatives |
| 8 | Process, plant and machine operatives | Factory workers |
| 9 | Elementary occupation | Bar workers, waiters, farm workers, postal workers, labouring work |

Activity

You may not have given much thought to which class you might belong to, before now. However, reflecting on what you have read so far and thinking about what we have discussed about class in strictly socio-economic terms, what class do you think you belong to?

You may find answering the first question quite difficult because the socio-economic definition of your class may seem to tell only part of your story. You may feel other aspects of your life, besides your earnings and your occupation or qualifications, have a bearing on which class you see yourself as belonging to.

For example, you may feel that the occupations of other members of your family, particularly if you go back one or two generations impacts on which class you identify yourself as belonging to. You may also feel that where you live has an impact on your class. From this activity we can see that class is not just about money, it is about identity too and from earlier chapters in the book we know that our identity is about sharing values, attitudes and beliefs with those around us.

Similarly, over the generations your family may have been *socially mobile*. That is, your parents may have, through education or employment, in social-economic terms moved into a different class to that of their parents. Similarly, you may be, in socio-economic terms, in a different class to your parents. Social mobility can mean moving from being working class to middle class and *vice versa*, and although we may move class we may still retain our original class identity. That is the values, attitudes and beliefs we were brought up with.

Read the following two case studies and decide in socio-economic terms and in terms of attitudes, values and beliefs which class those in the case studies belong to.

 Case study

Grace and Chamakomo have two children, Charity 3 and Imakando 6. The family come from Zimbabwe. In Zimbabwe Chamakomo was a teacher. He has a Zimbabwean teaching diploma, but it is not recognized in England so at the moment he works in a factory making plastic window frames.

Chamakomo is retraining to teach here, by 'topping-up' his diploma to a BA degree through studying part-time with The Open University. He then intends to do the one year's postgraduate qualification to get qualified teaching status. Grace works overnight shifts in a local care home. She would like to take up some training to get some qualifications as it is the only way she will be able to earn more, perhaps as a manager of a care home. At the moment getting Chamakomo qualified is the priority since he will be able to earn more and Grace still has the children to think about.

They are pleased to be in England because of the situation in Zimbabwe, and Grace worries about her mother who is still there. The family have moved three times in five years. At first they were in local authority bed and breakfast accommodation, Grace says: 'Those first two places were awful. In the first one we had one room for the family and we shared a kitchen and bathroom with other families, it was so dirty I'm sure I spent half my time cleaning up after others. Some of the people we shared with ... well, I used to think "and this is England?" We were lucky, Komo found work, although he was getting very depressed because he wasn't allowed to teach and we were all crammed into one room, which was so damp Kando kept getting chest infections, and with all the other families around it was never quiet. Luckily we had moved by the time Komo started studying.'

'Now we have much better accommodation (a two bedroomed flat with separate kitchen and living room), but I worry about the area. There are bad boys around here, and I don't want Kando to fall in with them and I worry that the school won't push him hard enough. We help him at home, but I think the work the school gives him is too easy. We don't let him talk in Shona at home anymore; he needs to make sure his English is perfect and get all the practice he can. I think it will be different when Komo gets qualified, we can move to a better area, with better schools and get a car! We had a car in Zimbabwe, but things are so expensive here we can't afford one at the moment. I miss our car.'

 ## Questions for discussion

What class do you think Grace and Chamakomo belong to?
What clues from the case study are you using to help you decide?
Are there any factors that are discussed in this case study that make it quite hard to say that Grace and Chamakomo belong to one class rather than another?
Are your decisions based on their income or their attitudes to life?

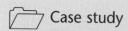 Case study

Charlie says: 'my dad passed the 11+ and went to grammar school. He came from Yorkshire and all his family, his parents, his aunts and uncles, etc. ran pubs for the local breweries, so accommodation came with the job. He grew up in pubs and was helping clean up and get ready for opening time from a very early age. After grammar school he went to university and then trained to be a teacher. Obviously this meant he could buy a house and had an occupational pension. Throughout his life he travelled widely and he sent all of us to university. However, he was a betting man all his life, always went down the pub on a Friday night, read *The Mirror* newspaper and watched football on Saturdays. He was very musical and when he was younger played in a band in pubs, but he thought the theatre and opera were overrated and for middle-class snobs.'

 Questions for discussion

What class do you think Charlie's dad could be described as belonging to?
What clues from the case study are you using to help you decide?
What are the factors in this case study that make it quite hard to say that Charlie's dad belonged to one class rather than another?
Are your decisions based on his income or his values, attitudes and beliefs?

## Low income, poverty, class and underachievement

One of the most complex issues to explore with regard to class, diversity, equality and achievement is the link between class and poverty. In Britain there has long been a concern for how best to provide for those who have no income or who are living in poverty. Indeed laws that state how the poor are to be provided for – or 'Poor Laws' – first appeared in 1598 (Social Policy, 2008). The current approach to trying to deal with poverty, particularly through what we now think of as 'the welfare state' began to emerge in the 1940s (Lund, 2002: 1), beginning with the Beveridge Report in 1942 (Lund, 2002: 107). Today we can expect the state to provide welfare for those who need it in the form of: social security (money for those who are currently unemployed or unable to work); free healthcare at the point of need; housing for all; free education; and other free welfare services for children (Lund, 2002: 107; Social Policy, 2008). However, despite available welfare support and free state education, we still live in a society that has families living in poverty. While there is evidence that shows that 'the proportion of people in "middle-class" jobs has increased' (Thomson, 2003: 167), and therefore arguably the number of families on higher incomes, other research indicates that the number of those living in poverty or on low incomes has risen over the past five years (The Poverty Site, 2009). Poverty can be measured in a number of ways. One way is through the notional 'basket of goods' that contain the items necessary for basic survival, food, shelter, clothing, etc. (Hills, 2004: 56), where those living in poverty are unable to purchase these basic minimum goods.

Poverty can also be measured by income, and those living in poverty are individuals who earn below the average national income or 60% below the median income. In the year 2006/07 the average income for those in work was approximately £24,000 a year and the median income was measured as being £19,600 (Blastland, 2008). Therefore, if we consider the median income, in particular, the statistics tell us that while 50% of incomes in 2006/07 were above £19,600, 50% of incomes were below £19,600 – remembering to also take into account that £19,600 is below the mean income of £24,000.

In the most extreme cases of poverty, children and families are not only financially poor but homeless too. Shelter's 2004 report about homeless children found that: 'at the end of December 2003, there were 95,060 homeless households' (Baker and Credland, 2004: 7). The report also says of these homeless households: 'around half … were pregnant women or families with children' and claims: 'people from different black and minority ethnic groups are over-represented among homeless households' (Baker and Credland, 2004: 7). It is likely, therefore, that schools, particularly those in deprived areas and areas of high diversity will have children who are homeless or may have experience of being homeless. Poverty and homelessness have considerable knock-on effects in terms of children's capacity to engage with their education. As Baker and Credland state homelessness can have: 'a damaging effect on the health and well-being of children and their families' (2004: 7).

 **Activity**

> In school the usual and only measure of children who come from low income families is achieved by counting the number of children who take Free School Meals (FSM). It is also worth bearing in mind that not all children who are entitled to FSM take up their entitlement to them.
>
> *(Continued)*

*(Continued)*

Think about children you have worked with who you know have FSM. While having FSM is a very public sign of low income, there may be other, less obvious aspects of their low income you might need to think about.

Children from low-income families and those who are homeless may also be dealing with a home life characterized by: 'poor amenities, overcrowding, lack of privacy, no safe place to play … [and] sharing a room with parents as well as older or younger siblings' (Baker and Credland, 2004: 9). Lack of privacy being a particular worry for children as they reach puberty and adolescence.

Children may also have nowhere to do homework and this may be even more difficult if space is limited and they are distracted by noisy brothers and sisters. The Shelter report also writes of children who: 'had been forced to get rid of pets when they became homeless, increasing their feelings of instability and insecurity' (Baker and Credland, 2004: 9).

 Case study

Daniel, who is five and lives on the outskirts of a large town in the north of England says: '… my mum doesn't make my packed lunches, they come in a special box, they're brought by a van everyday – I know 'cause I can see through the window when the van arrives and the man bringing the boxes in. Sometimes the sandwiches are OK, but you can't choose, you just have to have what is in that box. Sometimes I swap with Tom and sometimes the fruit is really yukky. They're OK [the lunches], but what I would like different is, I have to sit on a special table with others who have these boxes too. I want to sit with my friends, but the dinner ladies say "no, you have to sit here".'

 Question for discussion

What does this case study tell us about Daniel's experience of school as a child from a low-income family?

Education has always been seen as offering a way out of poverty and as we have already seen, logic would dictate that if education is free and available to all, then everyone has an equal chance to make their lives better through education. However, we also know that the link between simply attending school and achieving is not straightforward. We have already touched on the notion of social mobility, and for those who do achieve at school it is likely that they will have a better chance of enjoying well-being as adults, and throughout the rest of their lives. However, the research also shows that at the moment the biggest factor impacting on well-being in adulthood is background, a significant factor of which is class: 'people's occupational and economic destinations in early adulthood depend to an important degree on their origins' (Centre for Analysis of Social Exclusion, 2010: 25). The evidence the Centre for Analysis drew on to compile its report shows: 'the long arm of people's origins in shaping their life chances, stretching through life stages, literally from cradle to grave' (2010: 32). This is because the level of income a family has impacts on a child from their earliest years and can determine:

> ... opportunities such as the ability to buy houses in the catchment areas of the best schools, or to afford private education, with advantages for children that continue through and beyond education. At the other end of life, wealth levels are associated with stark differences in life expectancy after 50. (Centre for Analysis of Social Exclusion, 2010: 398)

## Class, values, attitudes and beliefs

When discussing poverty and low-income, and its relationship to class and equality of opportunity in education, one of the attitudes that always surfaces is the notion popularized by some aspects of the media that runs: there are those who want to live on benefit and are too lazy to get a job.

In real terms, when children first start school it is a very unusual child who cannot be engaged and motivated in some way to achieve in and enjoy their learning. As a child passes through its primary school experience it may become more challenging to motivate and interest. In part this will be because, as children grow up, very quickly there will be many influences on their life besides school. In Chapter 2 we saw how the notion of having an identity and identifying with those around us is important in helping us to develop a sense of self. When children begin to disengage with school, particularly at the primary level, it suggests that whatever is happening outside school is more interesting and motivating to them than what is being provided for them in school. They are finding it more rewarding to identify with these other influences than with school.

One of the reasons children begin to disengage with school is because the experiences they have at school do not connect with the way they live their lives or their experience of the world. 'Young people and their parents are influenced by the people and places where they live ... the local environment, crime rates and the quality of services, are ... likely to influence their attitudes (Cabinet Office, 2008: 15). In theory many seemingly disengaged children and parents accept that education does have an 'instrumental value' (O'Donnell and Sharpe, 2000: 4), but this does not necessarily translate into being able to engage with it. If the cultural background a child comes from, their family, friends and significant sectors of their local community believe that the 'real world' lies somewhere else other than school – which doesn't teach real skills and provides a curriculum remote from their daily experience – then it may seem increasingly pointless to engage with school.

As Adams, Bell and Griffin (2007) discuss, and we have discussed in previous chapters, some groups in society hold more economic and cultural power than other members of society and the dominance of those values, attitudes and beliefs can prevent others from thriving.

Earlier in the chapter we explored how some occupations, such as being a teacher, can be defined as a professional middle-class occupation. It may also be argued that these occupations are not only dominated by those who are economically middle class, but also culturally middle class. This in turn can set up barriers that prevent some children, particularly if they hold class values, attitudes and beliefs different to the class values, attitudes and beliefs prevalent in the school, from enjoying and achieving at school. There is, quite simply, a clash of values, attitudes, beliefs and experiences between some adults in schools and the children and families they are working with.

Generally the dominant class in terms of controlling what happens in schools is the middle class, those who have the professional qualifications to be teachers, head teachers and work in an advisory capacity in the Local Authority. Where the tension occurs is where those in control of the school have not reflected on their values and attitudes and can be certain that the community they work with shares the same values, attitudes and beliefs as they do. Lack of equality of opportunity for achievement happens where there is diversity in terms of class and the controlling class ignores the needs of the other, believing its way of 'doing things' is the more correct, 'better' way to enable children to achieve.

However, to believe that there is only one set of values which are the correct ones for achieving well-being is to be prejudiced and, to fail to acknowledge the complex issues most people deal with in their lives. It is also to assume that everyone has the same background and resources to draw on, lives in stable, safe communities with sustainable housing and has the financial capacity to plan for the future and survive unexpected events, like unemployment or redundancy. 'The ways in which social class affects educational opportunities are multiple and complex: some factors lie outside the school, others operate through institutional process that disadvantage particular groups of pupils' (Gillborn and Mirza, 2000: 19).

Let us take as an example the process of reading and learning to read. Schools invest a lot of their resources, time, effort and money in encouraging children and families to become involved in reading. It is a core element of the National Curriculum and general education policy that children become fluent readers and that they read for pleasure as well as for practical reasons.

The current National Curriculum requires children to engage with an extensive range of texts including literature (QCDA, 2010a). Research shows that teachers can have a tendency to interpret this as being a fairly traditional diet of British 'classic' fiction texts and poems, and contemporary authors that reflect the teachers' background and interests 'with teachers relying on the same texts over a lengthy period' (Ofsted, 2005a: 74).

The research also shows that teachers' interpretation of the literature aspect of the National Curriculum does not reflect children's interests and actually discourages children from reading for pleasure outside school (Ofsted, 2005a, 2005b). Indeed there is a 'dissonance between school reading and home reading choices and experiences' (Ofsted, 2005a: 9). When children are given the opportunity to talk about what does influence what they read most children cited friends as influences on their reading choices and 'fewer pupils mentioned that their reading had been influenced greatly by teachers' (Ofsted, 2005a: 24).

The research also finds that those children who most experience this dissonance are boys, and particularly boys from socio-economically disadvantaged backgrounds and ethnic minorities (Ofsted, 2005a, 2005b). This research (Ofsted, 2005a, 2005b) into children's reading habits showed that both boys and girls enjoyed reading comics and multi-modal texts for pleasure, neither of which were routinely used by schools to engage children in reading; indeed the children themselves said they thought teachers didn't approve of comics (Ofsted, 2005a: 9). This is an example of the dominant group – the teachers – deciding what it is best to use to encourage children to read without reflecting on whether they were correct or not.

Comics are not inherently bad, and as a way of motivating children to read might be shown to be good. The school's notion of what it is correct to read can be at odds with what the children actually read, and undermines the self-esteem of the child and family who will learn to 'accept and incorporate negative images of themselves fostered by the dominant society' (Adams et al., 2007: 11). This is not to say that the only thing children should read is comics, but to illustrate how children who may seem reluctant or not interested in the literature they are being given at school, must first be engaged in the reading process through texts they are familiar with and which do have interest for them. Once the children are engaged and can see that their interests are valued they can be introduced to a whole range of interesting and exciting texts (Knowles, 2009: 17).

We have already seen how it can be argued that British society provides equal access to all in terms of the benefits and advantages available in society, welfare support, health care and education. So, all have the opportunity, should they wish it, to achieve well-being. However, as we have also repeatedly seen, despite this seemingly level playing field, there are other factors at work that mitigate against some individuals being able to access these opportunities and flourish.

In this chapter we have explored how within British society, the class a child is born into will determine the long-term life chances of that child and how they are likely to enjoy and achieve in school. This is not necessarily because the child will be offered a poorer schooling than is available to all children, but because the values, attitudes and beliefs of those presenting the learning may be acting as a barrier to enabling the child to achieve.

Throughout this book we have seen how if we hold values, attitudes and beliefs different to those the children we work with it can affect the way we behave towards them, and however inadvertently, have an impact, positively or negatively, on their achievement. In most instances we want to have a positive impact on children's achievement. That we can be complicit in allowing some children to fail to achieve can be because: '... a dominant group can so successfully project its particular way of seeing social reality that its view is accepted as common sense, as part of the natural order, even by those who are disempowered by it' (Adams et al., 2007: 10).

## Activity

In terms of enabling children from diverse socio-economic backgrounds to achieve try thinking through some of the suggestions below and reflecting on how they might enhance your own practice.

What do you know about the socio-economic backgrounds of the children you work with, or have worked with?

When you are in school, or have been in school, is it obvious which children at school have Free School Meals? Are the FSM children treated differently at lunchtime or when the dinner register is taken, compared to the other children?

What do you really know about the area the children come from? Try not to take on face value things that might be said in the staff-room, do your own research. You can find out a lot about a place online through the Fischer Family Trust and the Index of Economic Deprivation (see list of websites at the end of this chapter).

Do you know where the parents of your children work? Who are the big local employers?

Talk to the children you work with, and where possible talk to their families. Find out what interests and motivates the children. Is it possible to personalize the children's learning to their interests?

As with your work with children from different cultures to the one you were brought up in, you may find that what the children want to explore is new to you, try researching the subjects for yourself. Read the books and other material they bring to school, find out what they watch on television. This does not mean you need to compromise the quality of the learning you are providing, it will simply give you some insight into how they view their own lives and may help you to better motivate some children to achieve in their learning.

## Further reading

- Barker, R. (1997) *Political Ideas in Modern Britain: In and After the 20th Century.* London: Routledge.

- Benson, J. (2003) *The Working Class in Britain, 1850–1939.* London: I B Tauris & Co Ltd.

- Cabinet Office Social Exclusion Task Force (2008) *Aspiration and Attainment Amongst Young People in Deprived Communities. Analysis and Discussion Paper.* London: Social Exclusion Task Force.

- Cannadine, D. (2000) *Class in Britain.* London: Penguin.

- Centre for Analysis of Social Exclusion (2010) *An Anatomy of Economic Inequality in the UK – Summary Report of the National Equality Panel.* Government Equalities Office.

- Department for Education and Skills (DfES) (2004) *Removing Barriers to Achievement.* London: DfES.

- Gillborn, D. and Mirza, H. (2000) *Educational Inequality: Mapping Race, Class and Gender.* London: Ofsted. Available at: http://www.ofsted.gov.uk/Ofsted-home/Publications-and-research/Browse-all-by/Education/Inclusion/Minority-ethnic-children/Educational-inequality-mapping-race-class-and-gender (accessed 05.08.09).

## Useful websites

- Fisher Family Trust: http://www.fischertrust.org/
  - An independent, non-profit organization which is mainly involved in undertaking and supporting projects addressing the development of education in the UK
- Shelter: www.shelter.org.uk
  - A charity that works to alleviate the distress caused by homelessness and bad housing
- The Poverty Site: www.poverty.org.uk
  - A site which monitors what is happening to poverty and social exclusion in the UK
- Index of Economic Deprivation: www.communities.gov.uk
  - The Index of Deprivation provides information about these areas of Britain that can be described as being deprived and how deprivation is measured.

# Boys, Girls, Gender Issues and Achievement

## Vini Lander

---

**This chapter explores:**

- The salient contemporary issues related to gender and education in Britain;
- The historical framework underpinning these issues;
- The prevailing myths about gender and provides counter-  arguments from recent research;
- The inter-sectionality of gender with other factors such as class and ethnicity.

---

This chapter may seem to be unnecessary in terms of the debate about achievement and gender because there is a popular assumption that the 'issue' of girls' achievement has now been resolved and that the issue now is boys' achievement. However, as we will see issues of inequality still exist in the classroom for both boys and girls. In order to better understand the debate it is helpful to move away from the polarized nature the debate can take – that is, of girls' achievement *versus* boys' achievement – and, rather to examine the complex factors which nuance the debate and the issues. It is important that those who work with children try not to be drawn into the polarized regions of the debate and appreciate the factors which influence achievement for some boys and for some girls. Please note we refer in the last sentence to achievement rather than underachievement. This is an important aspect of this chapter.

Defining the key issues and debates with respect to gender is not necessarily straightforward, since over the course of time the debate has changed from one which focused historically on whether girls should be educated or not, the nature of their education, the subjects they should study and their achievement within education, to the present time with the concern, almost panic, about boys' underachievement in comparison to girls' achievement. Yet, in the workplace women still do not enjoy gender equality or equal pay, despite equal opportunities and sex discrimination legislation. In all our discussions about diversity and equality, one of the aspects of the debate we have sought to explore is how there can often be a gap between the policy intended to address the issues raised and, what seems to actually happen in practice. This is no less true in terms of the gender and equality debate.

The area of gender and education illustrates how the gender debate has shifted over time. The recent heritage of the debate in Britain has enabled a considerable shift from the way gender roles, particularly for girls and women, were considered at the beginning of the twentieth century, to where we are now. Prior to the rise of the Suffragette Movement in the nineteenth century, and the raising of public awareness of the issues surrounding the unequal treatment, in all sectors of society, between girls and boys, or men and women, it was considered that girls were the 'fairer sex' or lesser sex. In part, in the West, this view of girls and women was supported by the Christian Church who propounded the notion of Eve as being the human more easily 'tempted' and the cause of Adam's failure to obey God. The eating of the 'apple of knowledge' in Genesis, the first chapter of the Bible tells the story of how Eve, through her succumbing to temptation and, in turn tempting Adam caused humanity to be dismissed from the Garden of Eden. In traditional Christian teaching the theme of women being temptresses is one that frequently reoccurs. Set against this propensity to be wanton and lead men astray is the teaching, particularly in the Letters of St Paul, that through being dutiful wives who obey their husbands women can, to a certain degree, redeem themselves. Interestingly, in other faiths, such as the Sikh religion, women are mentioned in the scriptures as equals and the first Guru of the Sikhs, Guru Nanak, opposed the prevailing view of women at the time as being inferior to men. He wrote that:

> It is through woman, the despised one, that we are conceived and from her that we are born. It is to woman that we get engaged and then married. She is our life-long friend and the survival of our race depends on her. On her death a man seeks another wife. Through woman we establish our social ties. Why denounce her, the one from whom even kings are born? (The Adi Granth 473 as quoted in Cole and Sambhi, 1978: 142)

This quote encapsulates the dilemma of womanhood – in the roles that women fulfil and the standing they have within society, whether it is a society from 500 years ago in India or modern Western society, where the dilemmas are in some ways the same and in others very different.

The following sections of this chapter outline the history of the debate about gender and education and how it plays out in the classroom; in the myths that prevail about gender and education; the nature of the teaching profession and how approaches to teaching and learning can begin to change thinking in classrooms with respect to gender and education. The section also examines the intersecting dimensions of gender, class and ethnicity.

## Gender and achievement – a historical perspective

The historical debate about women and education is rooted in the debate about their place in society in Britain. The perspective that we are presented about the role of women in society, through films and literature, is clearly classed. We have the image of the Victorian lady dressed in a fine gown having tea, playing the piano and 'as decorative, docile, delicate and dependent' (Browne and France, 1986a: 8), but this was an image of an upper-class privileged woman. The working-class woman would have to work and keep home in rather different conditions to her middle- or upper-class counterparts. But whichever class she belonged to the place of women in society has been cast as inferior, since the tasks of homemaker, cook and child carer were seen to be subservient to the role of the man as the major breadwinner (Browne and France, 1986a: 10). In fact, as Browne and France (1987: 10) note, in 1792 Mary Wollstonecraft, who could be considered a feminist in her time wrote that, 'The care of children in their infancy is one of the grand duties annexed to the female character by nature'. This perception can probably be traced back to cultural, geographical or religious origins, and Kumria (1987) notes that in almost every culture women are treated differently.

 Activity

The views you have about what the roles and responsibilities are for boys and girls and men and women will depend on your cultural heritage and the generation you come from. For example, your

*(Continued)*

*(Continued)*

parents' and grandparents' views on the subject may be different from yours. We also know from our exploration of identity in Chapter 2 that how we wish to portray ourselves as men or women is very closely tied to our sense of self.

The areas with regard to gender that are often contested, both by the media and in education, usually relate to the areas listed below. As you read through the list, consider your thoughts about each area of contention. Talk to your parents and grandparents about the issues. Talk to friends and colleagues who have a different cultural background to you to seek their views about the subject.

Ideas to consider:

- Are boys and girls 'born different', or does society expect different things from boys and girls, thereby seeming to create an artificial divide between the genders?
- Boys and girls should have the same opportunities in education, in terms of being able to go to school and study the same subjects in the same way. They should also have an equal entitlement to progress through the education system to higher education, if that is what the individual wants.
- Men and women should have the same entitlement in terms of wearing what they like and going out of the home to work if they wish.
- Bringing-up children is the responsibility of both men and women. Both should share in caring for and nurturing children in terms of meeting all aspects of children's needs.

The education of girls and women has always been inferior when compared to the education of boys and men. Mary Wollstonecraft was not only an early feminist, but an activist for social justice for the poor and women, and was brave enough to write against the slave trade. In 1787 she wrote a book entitled *Thoughts on the Education of Daughters* in which she criticized contemporary practice in the teaching of girls and the inadequacy of the curriculum at the time. In 1792, she wrote a now well known book called *A Vindication of the Rights of Woman*. It was a significant text at the time because it argued that women were not inferior to men and that it was their education and treatment in society which kept them in a state of ignorance and enslavement (Tomalin, 1992). Indeed Wollstonecraft set up schools herself to provide education for poor girls, while in Scotland the Church of Scotland and the work of John Knox contributed to establishing welfare and education for the poor.

Hargreaves (2004) notes that prior to the 1870 Education Act, education for girls was through free schools, such as the one set up by Wollstonecraft, which taught girls reading, needlework and knitting. It was after the Act that schooling was then available for girls at infant level within a co-educational setting and thereafter in single-sex provision. However, the curriculum involved subjects related to housework such as cookery and laundry. So the education provided for girls was a preparation for their lives as housewives, or for some as servants in the big houses of the upper classes. It should be noted that education for girls was not made compulsory until the age of 14 until after 1918. This increased the number of girls in secondary education but the curriculum remained essentially unchanged, with perhaps the addition of infant care. It should be noted that the education of girls was an issue raised by women in order to change the situation at the time, but the education of upper-middle-class boys was seen as of greater importance by the men in positions of power who could perpetuate their own classed and gendered beliefs.

So, the debate about the education of girls is inextricably linked to the perceived place of women in society, which in turn is influenced, in some societies, by religion. In the post-war years the schooling of girls was compulsory up to age 14 and then 16 but the curriculum for each gender was influenced by the perceptions of their future roles in society, which really had not changed much since the 1800s. In secondary school boys did woodwork, technical drawing and metal work, they could choose the sciences; whilst girls did domestic science, that is, cookery and needlework, and child care (Weiner, 1985). This distinction was even more marked between grammar schools and secondary modern schools. The girls in grammar schools probably had a greater choice of subjects but even they could not escape the clutches of domestic science. For whilst they may be preparing for entry to universities, even in the 1960s and 1970s the grammar school curriculum still offered domestic science as a compulsory subject up until age 14 as attested to by the author's schooling.

Gaine and George (1999: 63) highlight that although British law is enshrined in the rights of the individual 'it has never guaranteed basic human rights', and that it was a European Economic Community (EEC) directive about equal treatment of men and women which led to the Sex Discrimination Act in 1975. The Act outlaws discrimination on the basis of gender in the areas of employment, training and education (Gaine and George, 1999: 63). As Weiner (1985) comments, even the Sex Discrimination Act 1975 which dealt with equal pay for men and women did not include education within its scope of enforcement. Whilst there was a section related to education which outlined access to the curriculum on equal terms and that girls could not be discriminated against with reference to admissions to schools, there was little that related to discrimination on the basis of gender within schooling. So whilst boys and girls had equal opportunities and access to the curriculum, in fact there was little change with respect to boys and girls opting to take subjects and subsequently heading for careers based on gender related socialization.

This Act set up the Equal Opportunities Commission (EOC) which has now been subsumed into the Equality and Human Rights Commission. Weiner (1985: 2) notes that within the first 10 years of its existence there was not one case of educational discrimination upheld by the EOC and she argues that: 'this is not to say that there is no sex discrimination in education, but rather, that the existing legislation has proved ineffective in providing a basis for change in our schools'.

Weiner cites incidences of schools 'operating outside the law', noting that in the mid-1980s there was a different pass marks for boys and girls in local education authorities which still used the 11 plus exam for secondary school selection to ensure that there were equal numbers of boys and girls entering grammar schools. The 11 plus exam and the selective education system that it related to has largely diminished through the establishment of comprehensive schools, although there are still local authorities, such as Kent and Slough, that continue with a selective system based on examination results. However, the comprehensive system and the secondary curriculum, whilst allowing all children the choice of all subjects regardless of gender, has still been embroiled within a debate about gender and achievement.

 Activity

In talking to your family and friends ask them about any significant historical events which may have affected the perception of women in society in the twentieth century?

Can you see how these events have impacted, or not, on girls' education?

Are they reflected in the stories of education that your friends, mother or grandmother have told you?

What were the career aspirations of your parents' and grandparents' generation, particularly those of your mother and grandmother? How do your own aspirations match theirs? If you have a daughter, what are your aspirations for her?

So far the text has focused on the way society and the organizing structures of society have constrained the role and function of women in society and the home. But it should be noted that just as society assigned roles for women it conversely had certain expectations of men as the main wage earner, protector of his family, but not as the homemaker, the child carer or the cook in the family. But much has changed in this respect over the last 10 years and it is not unusual to hear of men staying at home to care for young children whilst their wife or partner works. However, it is still interesting that there are few men who choose to work with young children in a preschool or early years context. It could be argued that this is the result of a combination of reasons, such as: fear of being cast as effeminate and not 'butch'; fear of their interest in the care of young children being miscast or misconstrued; and the still prevalent reason that they 'didn't think that it was a man's job', which encapsulates the ever present belief of society that men are not expected to 'care' for young children. Yet we all know that as fathers that is exactly the role men take within their families. In the social sciences the term 'socialization' is used to describe how an individual acquires the norms, habits and expectations of a society. The main conduits of socialization are the family, schools, religion, peer group and the media.

 **Activity**

Think back to your own childhood and schooling. Can you identify key events, people or groups, books or media that influenced your socialization process?

Did such processes or events affect how you behaved as a girl or as a boy?

## Gender theory and gender relational theory

It is important that we move away from the dual or binary thinking that surrounds the discussions about girls and boys in schools. The way in which boys and girls behave is not entirely borne from their biology but from the way they are socialized in their family, school and society. Paechter (2001: 47) distinguishes between *sex* which is biologically determined, *gender assignment*, which usually occurs at birth and is based on the biologically expressed physical characteristics of a person, and *gender identity* which is defined as how a person feels about their own gender, which may be different to the gender assigned to them. *Gender role* is more complex. It is the performance of our gender which is constructed by the dominant discourses prevalent within society about what it means to be masculine or feminine. Such discourses are rooted in power and knowledge which has prevailed through time and we know that such power and knowledge is usually controlled by men. How we perform our gender role is dependent on the power and knowledge which prevails within the macro structures of society and the micro structures of family, school and peer groups. Our performance of gender roles is also dependent on our ethnicity and class.

## How do the issues of gender and achievement play out in classrooms?

### Gender and schooling

There are a number of issues and myths related to the education of boys and girls that are prevalent in the current education climate within England. These issues and myths will be discussed in the sections below in the light of the above theories. The first issue concerns the early years of education and how they can shape girls' and boys' socialization and the performance of gender in school and beyond. There are widely held assumptions that the curriculum within the nursery environment is 'gender neutral'. Browne and France (1986a: 146) assert that '*sexism* does occur in most nursery classrooms' since they are a reflection of 'society's perceived norms'. They consider three important mediums through which implicit messages are conveyed with respect to gender conformity: through the language used; teacher actions (or inactions); and visual images.

Epstein (1993: 10) examines how language is used for conveying our competing understandings of the world and suggests that the structure of the discourse and 'discursive practices' reveal the way in which constructed knowledge influences the way we are in the world. She argues that schooling not only identifies the nature of knowledge to be learnt but also the nature of what it is to be a child and a teacher and 'what it means to ... be gendered' (1993: 10). Gaine and George (1999: 36) strengthen the link between language and knowledge construction within society by noting that language 'acts as a vehicle for society's culture and social structure', adding how language can implicitly convey relationships of superiority or inferiority within a society. Browne and France (1986a) observed how language was used in a nursery classroom to reinforce gender stereotypes of girls and boys. For example, language was used to describe how pretty a girl looked, to compliment her for her dress and how the ribbon matched her dress, but conversely for boys if clothing was referred to it would be in terms of how comfortable it looked or in some other such reference to functionality. The use of the word 'little' was more frequently deployed to refer to girls than boys, apart from when parents and grandparents referred to boys as 'little man', however we rarely hear the term 'little woman' being used for girls. When comforting girls and boys different language was used for each gender; for girls the language was nurturing, warm and affectionate but for boys it conveyed a need to toughen up of the sort, 'big boys don't cry'. In a similar way it has been noted that the language used by parents, teachers and other adults to talk to children can reinforce societal gender expectations. So girls are expected to be 'lady-like', but not 'woman-like', other girls are referred to as tomboys and boys that may want to play with dolls or the kitchen in the home corner are called cissies, thus conveying that it is inappropriate for a girl to behave like a boy and be loud or assertive and it is inappropriate for boys to want to play at cooking, yet some of the world's greatest cooks are men who we call chefs. The weak girl who needs to be nurtured and cared for versus the strong tough boy are still prevalent stereotypes in many people's thinking and actions. Many children are conditioned into performing their gender long before they arrive at nursery school.

 Activity

Try this exercise. Ask a colleague within your school or setting to observe you for 10–15 minutes working with a group of children on four occasions across the day and on two randomly selected days in the week.

Ask them to note the occasions on which you use language to reinforce gender stereotypes and to note the phrases you use.

It is only through such self awareness and monitoring that we will become aware of how our own raced, classed and gendered socialization impacts within our own settings on our interaction with the children we work with.

The other way in which we are conditioned to perform our gender roles is through visual images and stories. Try to think of gender roles within stories, particularly stories of gentle princesses and brave princes. Can the children be encouraged to re-write it so that the prince is rescued by the brave and courageous princess? Browne and France (1986a) encourage teachers in nursery settings not to assign

Spot the dog a male gender; they ask why Spot can't be a female? For older children, are they presented with images of women as doctors, men as nurses and midwives, women as engineers and bus drivers and men as Early Years/nursery teachers or indeed at home caring for their children? If such images do not exist it is possible to create them yourselves by raising this question as a topic for debate with pupils.

The early years of life are where the socialization into gender roles occurs and it occurs not only through the way language is used but also the toys we buy for our children or give as presents at Christmas or for birthdays. How many times have you bought construction toys or cars for a young girl or a play set of kitchen utensils or a pram for a boy? Despite the positive images of young boys playing in the kitchen with such toys in colourful catalogues aimed at parents and Early Years practitioners, in the later years of primary schooling the work achieved to redress gender imbalance through play seems to reverse itself as games such as football or war/fighting games become more popular with boys. In fact, observe boys and girls in the play-ground at any primary school and you will find that the boys occupy the majority of the playground with their game of football, or are running around using the available space for their war game whilst the girls occupy a comparatively small proportion of the space with skipping games, talking or playing another game which does not take up all the available space. When such behaviours are observed it is easy but incorrect to assume that this is how boys and girls are, that this is what is to be expected.

 Case study

> Nina, a teacher in her late 40s in the north of England, says: 'when I was about three or four I was very interested in the "cowboy" films that were being shown on the television at the time. My parents went along with this interest and I remember having a cowboy suit and a rifle. I also remember wanting to play outside in the fields near where we lived and really did enjoy climbing trees. And yes, I was called a tomboy. As a teacher I have seen many young children exploring their gender roles, particularly in the early years, where boys and girls will use the home corner and role play areas to dress-up and try out different aspects of their identity. Many times I have seen boys wanting to dress-up as "princesses" and girls wanting to drive off to work. And then I see as the children get older they begin to be more gender "conforming" about the roles they take in imaginary games. When my son was little I painted his toenails for

him, as he wanted them done like mine and sent him off to nursery. My husband was mortified.'

 Questions for discussion

Would you paint a boy's toenails?
Why was Nina's husband shocked?
What are the hidden assumptions that may influence someone's reactions to painting a boy's toenails?

Teachers have a strong role to play in challenging their own thinking, the thinking of other professionals and of the children themselves to counteract the performance of expected gender roles in schools. If such counter-activity and thinking does not occur then gender stereotypical expectations will, and do, continue into the secondary phase.

## Who's achieving and who's not?

In the past issues related to gender manifested themselves at secondary level with respect to the subjects that pupils chose at age 14. But since English and mathematics have been compulsory subjects for public examinations for many years and science after the introduction of the National Curriculum in 1989, the debate with respect to the core subjects and pupils' relative performance within them has subsided a little except in the area of boys' reading and the rather panicked debate about the rise in the achievement of girls within a feminized curriculum. So what are the facts? The Department for Children, Schools and Families (or DCSF) (2010a) notes that when boys' results at age 16 are compared to that of girls of the same age that boys are found to be underachieving, that is there are not the same number of boys and girls achieving at the same level. However, it should be noted that not all boys are underachieving and that it is only in some subjects. Skelton et al. (2007) stress that it is important to note that the picture with respect to what is called the 'gender achievement gap' has become clouded with the focus on boys' underachievement. They advocate a nuanced picture which recognizes that there are some groups of boys who are achieving and that some groups of girls are underachieving. The latter seemed to get overlooked when the debate about boys' underachievement was raging at the start of the millennium.

Skelton et al. (2007: iii) note that girls do outperform boys in English and literacy by '10 percentage points in English at KS2 in 2006. However, there is almost no gender gap in achievement in mathematics and science at KS2'. They quell the panic by noting that such a gender gap in language is evident in other countries. DCSF (2009a) contends that although the achievement of boys and girls is broadly matched in mathematics and science at Key Stage 2 (KS2 age 11) the gap in English and literacy has been a longstanding phenomenon known since the 1950s and 1960s which was explained by the 'late development of boys' which did not in the long run affect educational outcomes.

## Teacher attitudes, teaching, learning and the curriculum

DCSF (2010) notes that there is evidence to suggest that teachers' gendered attitudes and expectations do affect 'pupils' perceptions of and reactions to school'. Also there is no evidence to suggest that male teachers are better for boys, and furthermore there is no evidence to substantiate a link between boys' achievement and the gender of their teacher (DCSF, 2009a). Indeed, some have stipulated that single-sex education benefits boys' achievement, but Ivinson and Murphy (2007) showed that where there was single-sex education it tended to benefit girls' performance and that this is a result of stereotypical teacher assumptions which in turn have affected their expectations of girls and their achievements.

Another myth which seems prevalent amongst the public and teachers alike is that the curriculum has become more feminized through the diminution of exams and the increase in course work. DCSF (2009a) outlines that the girls' results were improving prior to the change in course work requirements and that a reduction in the requirements had little effect on girls' results. The Ofsted report (2003a) on the achievement of boys in secondary schools noted that in schools where boys performed well there is a strong ethos of high expectations, clear boundaries for behaviour and more structured teaching and learning approaches which benefited all pupils.

## Gender, subject choice and careers

Whilst girls are achieving higher than boys in some subjects, in terms of subject choices post-16 there is the persistence of a familiar pattern, namely that there are still fewer girls choosing to continue studying science subjects than boys. This in turn affects career choices and paths since there are still more boys who study the sciences at Advanced level and go on to study the subject or related subjects in higher education. DCSF (2010) highlights that '60 per cent of working women are clustered in only 10 per cent of occupations; and men are also under-represented in a number of occupations'. There is an interesting debate about how boys and girls perceive different subjects. For example, some boys think that reading, writing and poetry are feminine modes of expression and that subjects such as science, maths, technology, PE and ICT are 'masculine' subjects whereas girls favour English, the humanities and other arts subjects. Whilst some girls are prepared to 'tackle' more masculine subjects the converse is not the case for boys (DCSF, 2010).

These perceptions of subjects being feminine or masculine are carried through to the career choices that youngsters make. For example DCSF (2010) acknowledges that girls still tend to choose careers in 'business and commerce, hairdressing, and beauty and caring services, while young men are still choosing engineering, construction and mainstream science subjects'. Skelton et al. (2007) argue that boys and girls tend to choose these different subjects because this is what is expected of them in terms of their gender performance, so girls choose English and the humanities but boys do not because this would run counter to their construction of being a boy. Therefore the myth of gender biased subjects is perpetuated through gender performance and teachers sometimes inadvertently, or perhaps not so inadvertently reinforce such expectations. So here again, in the twenty-first century, we have a pattern of subject and career choice which was prevalent in the 1970s and 1980s, despite the introduction of the National Curriculum which established equal access to all subjects up until the age of 16. This has not affected the subject choices or career paths of girls or boys in the last 30 years.

---

 **Activity**

Talk to a group of primary school children and find out which subjects they like and the reasons for their choice. Ask them what they would like to do after they leave school.

Think about the following ideas:

- Is there a pattern of gendered subject and career choices?
- If so point this out to the group. How do they explain the pattern?

## Intersectionality – ethnicity, class, gender and achievement

The pattern of achievement for boys and girls clearly differs but it would be a simple and essentialist stance to consider that gender is the only dimension of difference which affects the educational success of pupils in schools. The picture, as would be expected, is far more complex than the headlines reveal. It is not sufficient merely to consider the gender of each child when examining educational achievement statistics. This has been noted by Gillborn and Gipps (1996), Gillborn and Mirza (2000) and more recently by Skelton et al. (2007). The various studies cited suggest that:

1  When factors such as ethnicity are considered within the achievement debate it is clear that some groups of pupils achieve better than others, and when this is combined with gender then girls from all ethnic groups achieve better than the boys from those ethnic groups. Skelton et al. (2007) note that the average attainment for girls in English at Key Stage 2 was higher but there was a very small gender gap with respect to mathematics and science at this level.
2  Social class, in the case of the Skelton et al. (2007: iv) study, as measured by entitlement to Free School Meals (FSM), was a 'major impacting factor on educational achievement levels in the UK' for both girls and boys but the gap was greater for boys on FSM than those not receiving FSM.
3  Skelton et al. (2007: iv) note that the underachievement of pupils in lower socio-economic groups is a feature of the UK education system which is not reflected in the educational outcomes of children in Canada, Finland, Iceland, Japan, Korea and Sweden.
4  The nuanced picture (Mirza, 2009; Skelton et al., 2007) which takes account of gender, ethnicity and social class shows that social class has a greater effect on achievement than gender or ethnicity.

There are a number of possible explanations for these observed gender differences in attainment, as discussed earlier, but it is important to draw on the theoretical framework of gender relational theory (Skelton and Francis, 2003) which has been strengthened through empirical evidence which supports the theory that pupils' construction and performance of gender result in different behaviour for girls and boys which can impact on their achievement. The way in which girls and boys perform gender is dependent on the display of, and engagement in, behaviours which are 'different and opposite'

(Skelton et al. 2007: vi); in other words girls are expected to behave in ways which are different and the opposite of behaviours which define being a boy. These behaviours are rooted deeply in boys and girls and can vary according to age, social class and ethnicity. But it is clear that peer groups 'police' the 'gendered behaviours of their peers' (Skelton et al., 2007: vi) thereby reinforcing gender norms and expectations. These norms and expectations are defined by parameters which constitute masculinity and femininity. For example, it is not considered cool for boys to work hard at school which is regarded as feminine, so some boys, both working class and middle class are noted as demonstrating this behaviour (Skelton and Francis, 2003).

## Achievement, gender and family

Mensah and Kiernan (2010) in a recent research project working with the Millennium Cohort Study data found that boys' early educational attainment in communication, language and literacy was affected by their family environment. Their study did not take into account factors such as social class as signified by class categories or by FSM but used other factors to examine gender differences in educational attainment in the early years. They found that boys: 'in families of mothers lacking qualifications, living in poor quality areas or who had begun to have children at a young age were increasingly disadvantaged compared to girls in similar circumstances' (2010: 252).

They conclude that these gender differences are clearly affected by 'socio-cultural aspects of the family environment ... rather than by the family economic resources per se' extrapolating that boys in some way are more sensitive to disadvantages in their family environment and noting that other research has indicated that boys require 'greater external facilitation than girls' and this affects their learning. So any strategies to improve boys' educational achievement need to be put in place in the early years of education to counter the disadvantages evident within their family environment (Mensah and Kiernan, 2010: 253).

It is clear that there are a complex set of factors which affect the educational attainment of boys and girls. These factors, such as ethnicity, social class, peer group, family environment and teacher attitudes, intersect to act on an individual to influence their educational trajectory and future career and earning potential. Teachers need to be aware of these factors and actively work to counter them within their classrooms, setting high expectations regardless of the gender of all their pupils.

## Further reading

- Mirza H.S. (2009) *Race, Gender and Educational Desire: Why Black Women Succeed and Fail*. Abingdon: Routledge.

- Tomalin, C. (1992) *The Life and Death of Mary Wollstonecraft*. London: Penguin Books.

## Useful websites

- From History to Her Story: www.historytoherstory.org.uk
  - A major and unique project in women's history, examining through the lives and organizations of women the role they have played in history

# Coming from a Traveller Background: Gypsy, Roma and Traveller Children – Living on the Margins

## Vini Lander

**This chapter explores:**

- The history and origins of Gypsy and Roma people;
- The stereotypical assumptions about Gypsy, Roma and Traveller people;
- The educational debate related to children from Gypsy, Roma and Traveller heritages;
- The difference between Gypsy, Roma and Traveller groups;
- And challenges the reader's own positionality.

If there is one area of ethnic diversity which seems to raise more challenges than any other, it is that of Gypsy, Roma and Traveller peoples. Often they are seen as one homogeneous group which society labels as 'trouble-makers', 'crooks', 'dirty' and 'uncontrollable'. What is it about this group of people that evokes such strong negative reactions in an age in which we think that we are all equal? Why is it that people think it is all right to use the word 'pikey' but definitely not all right to use the n-word to refer to Black people?

This chapter will be thought-provoking. It will take you on a journey that will explain the history of the people from Gypsy, Roma and Traveller (GRT) heritages. The history of these groups is an ancient and proud one, perhaps not appreciated by 'ordinary' society.

The chapter will outline how legislation covers each group and limits their way of life. In setting this background we will examine issues related to schooling and the achievement of GRT pupils and how teachers and schools can support children from these cultures. Finally the chapter will conclude with a discussion about our own perspectives and how they can influence our engagement with issues related to GRT pupils in school.

## Mind your language

Just as Black and minority ethnic groups have helped to shape the terms used to refer to them so we must be mindful of the terms used to refer to Gypsy, Roma and Traveller people. The term Gypsy, Roma and Travellers is used extensively throughout this chapter usually in full but occasionally abbreviated to GRT. No disrespect is intended in such use. It is recognized that the term Gypsy, Roma and Traveller is merely an umbrella term and it should not be assumed that this is a homogeneous group. Previously in official documents the term Traveller was used simply because it described a group of people that had a nomadic lifestyle, but it did not affirm their separate ethnic identities. It is important that the language we use is inclusive and recognizes not only the ethnicity of each group but also the legal status afforded to the two main groups of 'Gypsy/Roma' and 'Travellers of Irish heritage' (DCSF, 2009d). In doing so we show respect for each group whilst also recognizing that the term may include other sub-groups. The term Gypsy encompasses many groups with tribal and geographical associations, for example, 'Vlach Rom', 'Rom', 'Kalderash', 'Siniti', 'Luri' and many other groups. It should also be noted that it is not acceptable to use lower case letters for the terms Gypsy, Roma or Traveller and that the word 'Gypsy' should be spelt with the letter 'y' rather than 'i' (DCSF, 2009d).

## Who are Gypsy, Roma and Traveller people?

The term GRT covers three main groups of people. It is interesting to note that it is a group of people that have been put together based on their way of life, one that has traditionally involved travelling from one place to another to earn money. If we examine this for a moment, at one time we were all travelling people in the way that many nomadic people live today, or try to live today. If we look at this in terms of the biological imperative that drives this movement from place to place it is clearly premised on survival, on using the natural resources in one area and moving on to give time for the renewal of these resources. In this way it was a sustainable way of life.

It is movement and migration that links the current Gypsy people with their ancestors in India. This link is not meant to imply that Gypsies are originally a nomadic people. It is estimated that there are 12 million Roma worldwide (www.reocities.com/~patrin/history. htm). There are no accurate records since this group does not feature on official census forms. It is thought that there are 300,000 Gypsy, Roma and Traveller people who have been in Britain for over 500 years. The Romany Gypsy people constitute the largest group of Travellers in Britain (www.multiverse.ac.uk), but the term Gypsy is a misnomer. The word Roma or 'Rom' means man or people. It is thought that the Roma people who are referred to by variety of other terms such as Gypsies, Tsigani, or, Zigeunerv, are descendants of warrior peoples from north India, possibly Rajasthan or the Punjab.

> It is unknown why the original descendants migrated west across from India to Europe between the ninth and fourteenth century. There is one theory that surmises they migrated due to the warring factions of Arab and Mongolian armies or that some such conflict dispossessed them of their homelands. Roma peoples travelled to Britain in the sixteenth century. Most Roma live in Central and Eastern Europe nowadays (www.multiverse. ac.uk).

It is mistakenly assumed that the Roma are referred to as such because they live in and come from Romania, but this is incorrect. The term Gypsy is thought to have been used by people in Britain who saw these dark-skinned strangers who they thought were pilgrims from Egypt, and so Gypsy is a corruption of the word Egyptian.

The theory about the origins of the Roma people and their migration is strengthened by examining the Romani language known as Romanes. The language has roots in ancient Sanskrit and is probably linked to Hindi and Punjabi. Many English Gypsies speak a version of Anglo-Romany or as it is known 'pogadi jib' (broken tongue) (DCSF, 2009d: 11). The Romani word 'kushti' which means good/nice could be related to the Punjabi and Hindi word 'khushi' which means happy or happiness. In fact some Romani words have filtered into common parlance through programmes such as 'Only Fools and Horses' for example, 'Mush, Pal, Posh, Bloke, Gaff, divvy, Lollipop, bamboozle, nark, Chavvy, put the mockers on' (www.multiverse.ac.uk).

We all use these words but have no appreciation of their origins.

The history of the Roma and Gypsy people is shaped and marred by the reactions of settled communities to the arrival of these 'strangers'. In fact there is no appreciation for their history and no trace of them in history as constituted by the dominant discourse. When the 'Rom' first arrived in Britain in the 1500s they were treated with suspicion. They were seen as a threat to the established faith, Christianity, because they were dark-skinned, a colour associated with the devil, with being a lesser mortal, being inferior; they practised palmistry and professed to be able to tell your fortune, a practice associated with the dark arts. So the foundations were laid for the preconceptions that prevail today, for example, the associations with superstition, wrong-doing and distrust. In fact Henry the Eighth and Elizabeth the First 'made it a capital offence to be a gypsy' (www. multiverse.ac.uk). The most reviled act of hostility is encapsulated in the statistic that half a million Gypsies were killed by the Nazis in their extermination camps.

Hostility towards Gypsy people these days seems to be rooted in this history of reaction against and control of the 'other', the stranger. It is thought that Roma and Gypsy people have remained nomadic due to this hostility since they have never been welcomed nor allowed to settle anywhere.

Many people may have a different image of Roma people as encountered in London and other European cities. A United Nations Development Program Report in 2003 found that there are about five million Roma living in Central and Eastern Europe and that 1 in 6 of these people face 'constant starvation' which has resulted from the negative treatment received by this group of people from the mainstream media, and neo-fascist groups. Many families have suffered racist attacks and even been murdered by racist thugs (www.multiverse.ac.uk). Since the Treaty of Accession of the European Union 2003 brought in 10 new European countries, including some from Central and Eastern Europe, persecuted Roma have fled to other countries in Europe to seek work as migrants and to escape racism, discrimination, hunger and poverty. Unfortunately in trying to escape racism in one country they have encountered it in others. For example, these Roma refugees have faced vilification even before they arrived in Britain with *The Daily Mail* in 2007 claiming 'Thousands of Roma Gypsies will head for the UK for a better Life' (www.dailymail.co.uk/newsarticle-481070/thousands-Roma-gypsies-head-uk-better-life.html); *The Daily Express* in 2004 under a map entitled the 'Great Invasion 2004' showed how the Roma would flood into and invade Britain. And in 2008 they claimed that Gypsy Roma would flood into Britain in search of jobs (www.express.co.uk/posts/view/33884/Roma-gypsies-head-for-good-life-in-Britain-after-they-are-told-get-a-job). The use of such emotive words as 'invade' and 'flood' are designed to cause alarm and inevitably create the notion of the 'other' as invading to plunder and take advantage of the majority's hard earned benefits. In this way the negative hype about Roma and Gypsy people is perpetuated. In a shameful incident of open racism in Northern Ireland in 2009 (Fox, 2009) the article notes that thugs attacked 20 Romanian Gypsy families by throwing bricks and bottles at their homes. The attacks were so violent that the families had to leave their homes and seek shelter in a church. The majority of these people were Roma and the youths that attacked them were seen to be making Nazi salutes. The article notes that such attacks have been seen across Europe and that Neo-Nazi groups in Italy have encouraged violence against the Roma.

The Traveller group is not a homogeneous group. It includes a range of people such as Gypsies, Roma, Scottish, Welsh and Irish Travellers and Show People such as circus and fairground people. Each group has its own specific heritage and history. Within the collective group known as Travellers are people who have their origins within Scottish, Welsh or Irish heritages. Originally they would have been itinerant workers or craftsmen such as metal workers and tinsmiths who would be known as tinkers. Derrington and Kendall (2004) surmise that Irish travellers may have been forced to take up this lifestyle during the oppression of Ireland by Cromwell or as a result of the potato famine, and indeed more recently in Ireland in 1963 the policy to force all travellers to settle in houses may have forced some to leave the country in order to maintain the travelling lifestyle.

Another group, known as fairground or circus showmen, distinguish themselves from Gypsies by considering themselves as travelling business people. Again this community has its own history which can probably be traced back to the days when holy days and feast days were celebrated with fairs where there was entertainment and trade. Many showmen families stay on their own or rented land, or live in houses during the winter and then travel around the country to a series of events. Their season is well planned to ensure a good income.

Another distinct group of travellers is the New Age Travellers and as the name implies it is a more modern cultural group. It is thought that this group probably started in the 1960s following the hippy culture and pop festivals of the time from venue to venue. More recently this group has also included people who have chosen to abandon a settled lifestyle to join environmental protest groups, or who have rejected the values of mainstream society to establish an alternative travelling lifestyle.

Case study

Background information:

The top of a road has been closed in the village because the family of an elder and respected member of a local Gypsy family has died. The road is closed because the family has erected a brazier in which they are burning things. The Roma believe that death and separation from loved ones anger the dying. This is why they do not leave a dying person on their own, there is always someone with them day and night and usually they are not left to die in the place in which they have lived. According to Gypsy tradition all the belongings of their relative must be burned in order to ensure there is no *marimé* or contamination from the deceased. Other Roma tribes believe that the deceased will need these possessions in the afterlife.

Imagine yourself as the proverbial 'fly on the wall' listening to the following conversation:

Terry:    I don't know why they have to have the road closed? If I started a fire in the road I would be in breach of some law wouldn't I? But they can have the road closed for them. They don't even pay taxes those Gypsies. They don't integrate into society, why do they have to be like that?

Mum:     Well it's their tradition and we should respect people's traditions. It won't be there for long and you have to admire people for holding on to their traditions even in this modern age don't you?

Terry:    I don't see why they have to inconvenience everyone. Why can't they burn it in the garden and anyway they'll leave a mess in the road and all the heat from that fire will damage the road.

Simon:  Why are you so racist?

Terry:    I'm not. I'm not racist but I don't see why they have to close the road and inconvenience people who live here. We have to go all the way round the other way.

Mum just holds her head in her hands; she thought that her son would have a more understanding attitude.

 Questions for discussion

What is your response to this conversation?
How would you help this mum out to make her son understand that essentially his attitude is racist?

## Travellers and settlers

In microcosm in Britain it should be noted that whilst we refer collectively to Gypsy, Roma and Traveller peoples as Travellers many of them are no longer nomadic travellers, but are settled and live in houses. So, teachers should be careful not to make assumptions when a child is identified as coming from a Traveller community. The erosion of a nomadic lifestyle has happened slowly over the years and was shaped not only by the reactions of mainstream society but by the instrument of the law. In the 1500s the Egyptians Act was passed to rid the country of people mistakenly thought to be Egyptians, namely the Gypsies. Another law at that time encouraged the Gypsies to abandon their ungodly way of life and settle in houses (www.gypsy-traveller.org). In each case the laws were accompanied by the threat of deportation or execution.

During the Second World War Gypsies worked on the farms since many men had been conscripted. At this time they may well have been tolerated since they were deemed to be contributing to maintaining the country's food supply. But after the Second World War the traditional work for Gypsy people, such as working on the land, gathering the harvest, or planting crops, diminished due to mechanization and the simultaneous industrialization of farming. These changes decreased opportunities for itinerant and seasonal work. At the same time the British landscape changed with the growth of towns and cities leading to urbanization and the passing of laws which restricted the use of land and thus for travellers restricted the legal stopping places they could access. Derrington (2004) writes that a law passed in 1960 'made it an offence for farmers to allow Gypsies to camp on their land'. In addition they could not purchase land to overwinter on unless they had a licence which needed to be gained through planning permission. This had the effect of forcing Gypsy Travellers to camp on roadsides. In 1968 the Caravan Sites Act stipulated that local councils had to provide accommodation or areas for Gypsies to stop while other areas could be designated sites which were inaccessible to Gypsies and further still if they were to stop on such land it would be a criminal offence. There were a minimum number of official pitches provided and residing on such pitches came with rules such as no trading and no keeping of animals. This had three major effects: firstly to drive Gypsy Travellers to other areas; secondly to limit their income since they could not trade from their pitches whereas this had been their traditional way of conducting business; thirdly and most importantly the restricted number of pitches served to break down the extended network in which families travelled. Also it restricted the family functions such as gatherings for marriages and deaths, so affecting Gypsy cultural traditions.

The erosion of the Gypsy lifestyle has continued in more recent times. The 1994 Criminal Justice and Public Order Act repealed part of the 1968 Act which required local councils to provide sites for

Gypsies and Travellers to stay on. This was accompanied by the removal of the grant that enabled councils to build such sites. It increased the powers of police and councils to evict Travellers camping illegally by the roadside and if the Travellers refused to move they could be arrested and prosecuted. Indeed this law was draconian when used in conjunction with the Public Order Act 1986 which gave the police power to remove people who trespassed on land or if they had six or more vehicles. This law also applied to encampments on roadsides. Such laws left Travellers with nowhere to turn since councils did not have to build sites and in the 1980s and 1990s could close down existing sites, in some cases selling them off for housing developments. In fact Travellers can buy land that they can use as sites and some have done so, but in reality this is also difficult due to the process of applying for planning permission and local opposition. In effect the law has served not only to radically affect the life and traditional culture of Gypsies it has served to *criminalize it* (www. gypsy-traveller.org). This is why many Gypsy people are settled living in houses or on council or privately owned sites, perhaps in static caravans. Often council sites or private sites are in inaccessible or in less desirable places such as close to railway lines, rubbish tips or sewage works. They can be miles from a road and accessible only via muddy tracks. Those that live on council sites have to pay rent for the concrete on which they park their trailers and they have to pay council tax but they do not have access to the same amenities as people who live in houses.

Interestingly, the responsibility for the oversight and management of Travellers' sites falls under the remit not of the local council housing department but of the Environmental Health department. This is the department that deals with unhealthy, unclean issues, the department that deals with the extermination of rats and vermin. Is it surprising that some members of society continue to make the false assumption that Travellers are unclean and unwanted? Indeed, it is not surprising then that those who are forced to physically live on the margins of society are also metaphorically thought of and treated like detritus by society.

---

 Activity

Mary, a primary student teacher is a bit confused. She has a new child in her class, Danny, who is a child from a Traveller background but lives in a house not far from the school. She wonders why he is still referred to as a Traveller.

*What do you think?*

For example, in the new topic entitled 'Houses and Homes' should she include pictures of trailers and caravans regardless of whether she has got Gypsy, Roma or Traveller children in her classroom? Or should she do it now she has Danny in her class?

To assume that a child's identity is based on the locality of their homes is to deny their cultural heritage which remains the mainstay of their lives regardless of whether they live in a trailer or a house. So the answer is that they still ought to be referred to by their ethnicity. It is not their abode that determines their identity but their ethnicity and culture. It is this ethnicity which drives their language, traditions and customs, whether they live in a house, a static trailer or choose to travel at some times of the year. It is the ethnicity and culture of this group that should be reflected in the classroom. Because they are following a more static way of life, this does not mean that they are no longer Gypsy, or Roma or Travellers.

Whilst the law has not outlawed the nomadic way of life it has served to restrict it. It seems that the nomadic lifestyle, to move around and not be settled in a static home, seems to challenge the normative framework of values that mainstream society adheres to and promotes. Such values are embedded in our reactions to the 'other', to their way of life as a less sociable way of existence, and one that does not suit us. Through the law and rejection we appear to 'bring into line', or 'normalize' the 'other' and their way of life.

## We are all equal except some are more equal than others

The continued stereotypes of Gypsy, Roma and Travellers and children is one of outcasts, as not belonging, dirty, a nuisance at the very least, criminals and thieves at the very worst. The stereotype of being dirty could not be further from the truth. Gypsy Traveller people are proud of their trailers and keep them in an immaculate condition. Their children are seen as unruly and some would say uneducable. Again, such myths are just that. It is these negative stereotypes that perpetuate the ongoing prejudice and racism faced by Gypsy, Roma and Travellers. This discrimination has denied them access to many provisions. For example, their children have the right to access education without fear of prejudice or to be subject to the deficit model of learning which operates in some educational establishments. Despite the fact that Gypsy, Roma and Irish travellers are recognized as a distinct ethnic group and so covered by the Race Relations Amendment Act (2000), direct and indirect discrimination continues to affect the lives of youngsters in school and their families. Although we no longer see signs, as we did in the 1960s, saying, 'No Blacks, No Irish and No Dogs', unfortunately you can still see signs on pubs or clubs saying 'No Travellers'. This is, of course, illegal. Yet it is ignored, there is no public outcry and it appears to be silently accepted. In 2003 the BBC reported that a 14-year-old boy, John Delaney, was kicked to death by two teenagers because he was from a Traveller family. The teenagers claimed he deserved it he was 'only' a gypsy (BBC, 2003).

In the climate of a history of rejection it is not surprising that many children from Gypsy, Roma and Traveller families do not achieve in school.

---

 **Activity**

As you sit in the staffroom you hear a teacher whom you admire as a good practitioner say the following about a Gypsy family in the school, 'I don't know why they carry on having so many children. Can't they stop?' You were under the impression that this colleague was a tolerant, liberal person.

What would you do? Should you say something or carry on eating your sandwich?

It may be that you want to say something, but do not know how to begin, or what to draw on to support what you want to say. You may not feel you have the right strategies to disagree with a colleague over such an issue.

In terms of suggesting an alternative viewpoint to someone, the first thing you might want to do is to do further research about the issue, to give you the confidence to counter what is being said.

Good opening sentences for beginning these sorts of discussions are: 'I hear what you are saying, but I think ...'

'Yes, I have heard other people say that, but actually ...'

---

## Equality and achievement – how do schools and teachers support the education and well-being of Gypsy, Roma and Traveller pupils?

So far this chapter has focused on the issue of systemic racism and discrimination that has affected the history and lives of people from

Gypsy, Roma and Traveller backgrounds. It is not until we, as members of the 'mainstream community' and teachers within it, recognize and acknowledge the negative factors that children from Gypsy, Roma and Traveller communities have endured and the reasons why they have existed on the margins of society that we will begin to understand why this can no longer continue in an age when Every Child Matters. It is the schools' and the teachers' legal and moral duty to promote the education and well-being of pupils with Gypsy, Roma or Traveller heritages.

The underachievement of pupils from GRT groups is not a new phenomenon. It was noted in a HMI report in 1971, and mentioned in the Swann Report *Education for All* in 1985, where the report acknowledged that the extreme prejudice and alienation suffered by 'Travellers' children' was also evident amongst children from BME groups. More recently the Ofsted Report (2003b) *Provision and Support for Traveller Pupils* highlights the major concerns about access to education for Traveller children and schools' duty under the Race Relations legislation. It notes how in the past 'the alarm bells rung in earlier reports have yet to be heeded' (2003b: 6). The report also indicates how Traveller children make good progress in lessons but that the attainment gap widens as they get older. It commends the work of local authority Traveller Education Support Services (TESS) but highlights some major failings:

> All local authorities are responding to the requirements of the Race Relations (Amendment) Act. In one in four authorities, the Traveller education service had made a significant contribution to this work. Many authorities have clear statements about the inclusion of all pupils in education. However, in too many authorities, the ways in which they deal with unauthorised encampments contradict the principles set out in their public statements on inclusion, educational entitlement and race equality. Such contradictions undermine relationships and inhibit the effectiveness of the Traveller education services and other agencies. (Ofsted, 2003b: 5)

The report also highlighted the issue of Travellers not ascribing their own ethnicity on ethnic monitoring forms, the lack of Traveller culture reflected in the curriculum since they are not seen to be an ethnic minority and that Traveller pupils remain on the periphery. The statistics for the attainment of Gypsy, Roma and Traveller pupils show that 49.5% of Gypsy, or Roma pupils and 52% of children with Irish Traveller heritage 'are in the bottom 20% of the Early Years Foundation Stage' (DCSF, 2009d). From this starting point the gap continues to widen at Key Stage 1 and at Key Stage 2 where 40% [81%] of children from Gypsy or Roma families attain Level 4 in English whilst 33% of those from Irish Traveller heritage attain the same level in English. The percentages given in [ ] brackets show the attainment of all pupils (DCSF, 2009d). At secondary level only 15.7% [63.5%] of pupils from Gypsy/Roma heritages gain five GCSEs at grade A*–C and 17.4% for Traveller pupils of Irish heritage. Whilst 98.2% of all pupils attain GCSE passes at grade G or above only 71.6% of pupils from Traveller Irish heritage backgrounds gain the same GCSEs and 84.4% of Gypsy/Roma pupils gain GCSEs at grade G and above. The recent DCSF National Strategies materials on raising Gypsy, Roma and Traveller achievement note that:

> ... the DCSF is able to identify trends and gaps relating to a number of educationally significant factors, such as rates of achievement and attendance, identification of special educational needs (SEN) and rates of exclusion. This data monitoring enables the cross reference of other factors that contribute to underachievement, such as eligibility for Free School Meals (FSM) among these communities. In this regard it is significant to note that these poverty indicators are only marginal contributors to the underachievement of Gypsy, Roma and Traveller pupils; the causes of their underachievement lie beyond these factors. (DCSF 2009d: 14)

The excellent materials published by DCSF (see Further Reading) outline some of these other factors, for example that some schools, despite their legal duty, have discriminated against this group by refusing school places to children from Gypsy, Roma and Traveller communities. Other schools, for whatever reason, have offered limited places, so seemed to be unable to offer places to siblings. Gypsy, Roma and Traveller parents have rightly wanted to keep their children together for reasons not just of having support and solidarity from their siblings but just like any other parents from their strong feelings of responsibility and care for their children. Many GRT parents have probably been very wary of schools, based perhaps on their own negative experiences in the past. It should be noted that children in Gypsy, Roma and Traveller communities are respected, loved and cared for by their parents, who want, just like any other parent, to protect their children from harm which can; in some situations, come in the form of racist bullying (Derrington, 2004).

In a very honest reflection on her own education and upbringing, one teacher with a Gypsy heritage (Multiverse, 2009) writes how she kept her identity hidden whilst she was training to be a teacher and now as a teacher in school. This reflection sums up how even in today's so-called tolerant society not everybody feels that their identity is one which will be equally valued.

As teachers and educational professionals it is important that we are aware of our own perceptions and of the assumptions we may make about individual children and their families. It is these assumptions and perceptions which may implicitly affect the way we work with some children, their parents and other colleagues. It is our dedication and commitment to the well-being and achievement of the children and our engagement with issues of equality in real classrooms that will make a difference to the lives of the Gypsy, Roma and Traveller pupils in our schools.

## Further reading

- Bhopal, K., Gundara, J., Jones, C. and Owen, C. (2000) *Working Towards Inclusive Education: Aspects of Good Practice for Gypsy Traveller Pupils*. DfEE Research Report No. 238. Norwich: DfEE.

- Bhopal, K. and Myers, M. (2008) *Insiders, Outsiders and Others: Gypsies and Identity*. Hatfield: University of Hertfordshire Press.

- Department for Children, Schools and Families (DCSF) (2009) *Building Futures: Developing Trust: A Focus on Provision for Children from Gypsy, Roma and Traveller Backgrounds in Early Years Foundation Stage*. Nottingham: DCSF Publications. Available at: www.standards.dcsf.gov.uk

- Department for Children, Schools and Families (DCSF) (2009) *Moving Forward Together: Raising Gypsy, Roma and Traveller Achievement. Booklet 2: Leadership and Management*. Nottingham: DCSF Publications. Available at: www.standards.dcsf.gov.uk

- Department for Children, Schools and Families (DCSF) (2009) *Moving Forward Together: Raising Gypsy, Roma and Traveller Achievement. Booklet 3: Learning and Teaching*. Nottingham: DCSF Publications. Available at: www.standards.dcsf.gov.uk

- Department for Children, Schools and Families (DCSF) (2009) *Moving Forward Together: Raising Gypsy, Roma and Traveller Achievement. Booklet 4: Engagement with parents, carers and the wider community*. Nottingham: DCSF Publications. Available at: www.standards.dcsf.gov.uk

## Useful websites

- Scottish Traveller Education Programme (STEP): www.scottishtravellered.net/
  - o Based at The University of Edinburgh and funded by the Scottish Government, its remit is to support developments in inclusive educational approaches for Scotland's Travelling Communities

- Friends, Families and Travellers: http://www.gypsy-traveller.org/
  - o Seeks to end racism and discrimination against Gypsies and Travellers, whatever their ethnicity, culture or background, whether settled or mobile, and to protect the right to pursue a nomadic way of life

- Multiverse: www.multiverse.ac.uk
  - A website for teacher educators and student teachers addressing the educational achievement of pupils from diverse backgrounds
- National Association for the Teachers of Travellers + Other Professionals: www.natt.org.uk/
  - The association was established to address the isolation of teachers of Travellers and to support and encourage their work
- Teachers TV: www.teachers.tv
  - A website with engaging videos, practical resources and an active online community to encourage teacher development

# Refugee and Asylum Seeker Children

## Vini Lander

> ### This chapter explores:
>
> - The distinction between the terms refugee and asylum seeker;
> - How the experience of refugee and asylum seeking children may impact on their learning and achievement in school;
> - How schools and teachers can support the well-being of refugee and asylum seeker children through understanding the wider needs of their families.

The particular educational needs of refugee and asylum seeking children is an area which is perhaps the least recognized and acknowledged within schools. This could be because the issue may be confined to certain schools in certain areas of Britain, for the simple reason that refugee and asylum seeker families are settled in certain areas. Therefore it is an issue which may be quite removed from the consciousness and experience of many student teachers and teachers. However, the national consciousness is affected by negative headlines in newspapers which indicate that there are too many people in England seeking refuge. It should be noted that people who are referred to as asylum seekers or refugees are not the same as economic migrants. People in the former categories are fleeing persecution, conflict and war, whereas economic migrants will have planned their stay in Britain and will still have a home and safe place to return to in their own country, when and if they decide to return.

That refugees and asylum seekers are, as the term suggests, in fear of their lives in the country they have come from, highlights a number of inter-related issues that impact on the education of refugee and asylum seeker children. For example, there are issues related to their emotional well-being, language, religion and ethnicity which are overlaid by legal issues related to their status and applications to stay in Britain. These issues affect the children and their families. But some children may be in Britain on their own as a result of their families trying to find a better life for their child whilst they may remain in their country of origin which may be affected by war, or by political or ethnic tension and violence.

The needs of these children and their families can also be complex, requiring the support of a number of services such as housing, medical, education and sometimes social services. Most refugees and asylum seekers arrive in Britain with very few possessions and nowhere to live and sometimes no family with them or no family to live with. Their plight is not to be envied but considered with compassion and understanding. For example, fleeing your home country, leaving behind your extended family, house, possessions to become dispossessed is not a decision any father or mother makes lightly. It is only when their freedom and rights are severely restricted or their lives are in danger that they decide there is no alternative but to flee. As one young man said: 'No-one chooses to be a refugee' (http://www.teachers.tv/videos/refugee-kids).

## Case study

Abdi is a 14-year-old boy who has just arrived as an unaccompanied asylum seeker. He has just landed at Gatwick Airport, London. The Immigration and Border Control Officers take him to an interview room. Abdi appears tired, confused and bewildered by his surroundings. He was told by his uncle that there would be a better life for him in England. But it has been two months since he last saw his family and his village. It was then that the men with guns ran amok in his village shooting and killing anyone they saw. They murdered his father, mother and big brother. He had seen this all from his hiding place. After the sights he had seen he ran to the next village to tell his uncle. His uncle took him to the capital of Somalia and handed him over to a man. The man took him to Mogadishu airport and put him on the plane. Abdi didn't know he had a passport until then. Now he is in a room with a man who is asking him questions. He seems all right and Abdi can ascertain that he probably wants to know why he has come to England but Abdi can't tell him because he doesn't speak English.

Questions for discussion

What do you think are Abdi's immediate thoughts and feelings? Imagine yourself in his position, or imagine your son or daughter in this position. How would you like to see them supported?

This is how the story of some children's lives as an asylum seeker in England can start. They arrive unaccompanied and sometimes they know why they have left their families behind, sometimes they don't. On arrival another phase of their life journey begins to unfold, a phase that they have very little control over. Every year 3,000 unaccompanied children under the age of 17 arrive in the UK and apply for asylum (http://www.multiverse.ac.uk/ViewArticle2. aspx?Keyword=asylum+seekers+and+refugees&SearchOption=And &SearchType=Keyword&RefineExpand=1&ContentId=15499).

As you can imagine life must be pretty awful for a parent to send a beloved child on such a long and unknown journey and to trust the future of their child to strangers. To develop your understanding of the complex issues faced by these children you are advised to read Benjamin Zephaniah's (2001) book *Refugee Boy*.

## History and definitions

The 1951 Refugee Convention was designed to tackle issues of refugees after the Second World War and as such applied largely to a European context rather than a global one. The Convention was modified by the 1967 Protocol which extended its application across the world. It is known that 147 states have signed up to the Convention and its Protocol (UNHCR, 2007). The Convention and its Protocol obliges host states to protect refugees. Although written in 1951 for a very different world situation, 'the Convention has proved remarkably resilient in helping to protect more than 50 million people in a wide variety of situations' (UNHCR, 2007: 9). Can you think of recent situations across the world in which the Convention and its Protocol would apply?

The Convention was the first international agreement to define the basic human rights of refugees. It defines who is and is not a refugee (for example, war criminals are not considered refugees) as well as their right to protection and services from countries that have signed up to the Convention. It defines the rights of refugees, for example, their rights to freedom to practise their religion, to freedom of movement and their right to work and education. It also states that no country should return refugees to the country of origin if they fear persecution. People who are fleeing conflict in one area of the country but stay within the borders of the country, for example, Tamils in Sri Lanka or the people of Dafur in Sudan are referred to as Internally Displaced People. In this situation the Convention and its Protocol do not apply. To be referred to as a refugee you must cross an international border from one country to another. It is interesting to note that one stops being a refugee when you have gained the right to permanently reside in the country in which you first sought asylum. The preferred option is that refugees return to their country of origin when it is safe to do so. This was the case when thousands of Rwandan refugees returned home after the genocide in 1996. It should be noted that under international law no country can return a refugee to their country of origin if they are still in danger of persecution (UNHCR, 2007). The idea promulgated by the popular press of asylum seekers flooding the country is a common myth which deserves to be extinguished. UNHCR (2007) notes that the idea of asylum seekers swamping some countries is not borne out by the facts:

> Countries around the world, including some in Europe, believe they are being overwhelmed by asylum seekers. The global number of asylum seekers did increase in the 1980s and 1990s, but then decreased sharply during the first years of the new millennium. The concerns of individual states are relative. The bottom line is that some nations in Africa, Asia and the Middle East – states with far fewer economic resources than the major industrialized countries – sometimes host much larger numbers of refugees over much longer periods. (UNHCR, 2007: 16)

In fact under 14% of the refugees in the world live in Europe (www. refugeecouncil.org.uk). It may be worth remembering this rather small figure when you read alarmist headlines or negative comments about refugees.

## Definitions of the terms asylum seeker and refugee

The two terms are often used interchangeably but it should be noted that in law they are different. In common parlance we do not distinguish between the two terms. But there are differences which teachers and education professionals should appreciate.

## Definition of the term asylum seeker

> An asylum seeker is a person who has crossed an international border in search
> of safety and refugee status in another country. The person and dependents
> have applied for asylum. In the UK asylum seekers are people who are awaiting
> a Home Office decision as to whether they can remain. (http://www.multi-
> verse.ac.uk/viewarticle2.aspx?contentId=15422)

As noted earlier, the 1951 UN Convention and 1967 UN Protocol
define the rights of asylum seekers. A person can declare themselves
to be seeking asylum when they arrive at an airport or port. They
can also declare themselves as such when they are in the country.
The Home Office has a special department, called the Immigration
and Nationality Directorate (IND), which processes all the applications for asylum. The person who has declared themselves as an
asylum seeker is required to complete an application which should
be supported by evidence. The IND then assesses the evidence and
the claim. Rutter (2003) notes that this process can have one of four
outcomes:

1  The claimant is assigned refugee status because there is evidence
   to show that there is a 'well founded fear of being persecuted for
   reasons of race, religion, nationality, membership of a particular
   social group or political opinion' (UNHCR, 2007: 6);
2  The applicant is granted 'Humanitarian Protection' but is not
   given refugee status. This protection covers a period of time and
   recognizes that if returned to their country of origin the person
   would be in danger of torture or being killed;
3  Discretionary leave is granted to people who are not granted asylum and cannot be returned to their country of origin. This is
   often granted to unaccompanied children who have not been
   granted refugee status and who are under 18;
4  About 80% of applications are refused. Applicants whose claim is
   refused may have the right to appeal but only 25% are successful.

Forty-three per cent of people seeking asylum come from one of
the following countries: Iraq, Zimbabwe, Afghanistan, Somalia and
China, and smaller numbers from other countries such as Sri Lanka
and the Democratic Republic of Congo. The political situation in
each of these countries is widely known and violations of human
rights are reported in our news. Most people seeking asylum are men
between the ages of 18 and 34. Three thousand unaccompanied children under the age of 18 apply for asylum each year. People who
apply for asylum cannot work but require care, support and housing.

Rutter (2003) notes that asylum seekers do not have access to state benefits but children from asylum seeking families can access schooling. The National Asylum Support Service provides financial support and housing. They operate a policy of housing asylum seekers anywhere in the country in an attempt to control the numbers in London and the South East of England. This may sound straightforward but an asylum seeking family can be moved many times to different areas of the same city or region or to different parts of the country. This has the inevitable consequence of adding to their stress and insecurity. The children have to move schools as many times as they move home.

## Definition of a refugee

Rutter (2003) notes that the term is more a 'legal construct' which defines a refugee as 'someone who has fled their own country or is unable to return to it owing to a well-founded fear of being persecuted for reasons of race, religion, nationality, membership of a particular group or political opinion' (1951 UN Convention Relating to the Status of Refugees). Under the 1951 UN Convention Relating to the Status of Refugees and its 1967 Protocol, the country in which the person seeks refuge can deem the person to be a refugee. Usually people will seek asylum and make an application, and, if successful, they will be granted refugee status. This status affords people the protection of the state in which they have sought sanctuary and protection from being returned to their country of origin. It also means that people with refugee status can work, have access to benefits, housing, medical care and education. A small number of asylum applications gain refugee status – only 6% in 2003. In 2009 the UK was home to only 2% of the 16 million refugees worldwide (refugee-council.org.uk). The most successful group of refugees in Britain are the Ugandan Asians that were expelled by President Idi Amin in 1972 (www.refugeecouncil.org.uk).

Rutter (2003) explains that whilst in law the status of an asylum seeker and refugee are clear, schools tend not to delineate or know the difference, or even ask. This is because the journey which describes the flight of asylum seekers and refugees from their countries of origin are not straightforward. They can often gain asylum or refugee status in one country and then migrate to another. Remember 80% of the world's refugees are in camps or housing in countries within Africa or the Middle East, countries such as Kenya or Jordan or Syria. So, for example, if you gain refugee status in Sweden as a Somali asylum seeker you may then later come to the UK. In this case the children may speak Somali, Swedish and depending on their age they may also have learnt English in Sweden.

It is estimated that there are 100,000 refugee children in the UK and that about 65% are found in the Greater London area. The largest proportion of refugee children in schools is from Somalia and the numbers indicate that approximately 6% of children in London schools are from refugee backgrounds (Rutter, 2006).

 Case study

Farrah and her mother arrived in Dover after an arduous overland journey from Iraq. Farrah is eight and she is really not sure what has happened to her father. She just remembers being told they were visiting her grandmother and she was put in the car for what she thought was a weekend trip. Her memory is hazy because she was half asleep and half awake as they made their way through the countryside, then on via Syria and other countries to Britain. She hears mum talking to an interpreter and she hears her tell her that they are seeking asylum.

Farrah and her mother are given accommodation in a detention centre where there were many people from around the world. They were then moved to Croydon where they had a small flat. Farrah's mother told her she didn't know how long they would be there but they would try to get her into a school, which they did with the help of a neighbour who was also from Iraq. She was at the school for just half a term and they got moved to North London where it took her mother four months to find a school for Farrah. They spent their days watching television and in that way they started to learn more English. Farrah's mother cried a lot and sometimes she shouted at Farrah, especially if she was messy in this new very small flat. There were very noisy neighbours above who were quite hostile. Farrah is now in her second school in Britain in six months. She asks after her father almost every day and over the course of the days and now the months the answer has moved from 'he will be with us soon', to 'I don't know', and sometimes her mother cries and other times she stares out of the window as if willing him to appear.

 Questions for discussion

As someone who works with Farrah, how would you make Farrah welcome in your classroom?
What would you want to know about her?
How could the school support this family?

This case study provides a very small sample of the issues met by asylum seeker families and their children. They are often families that are emotionally stressed and who are trying to do their best for their children, as any mother or father would seek to do. Schools can support such families by ensuring that they have access to the relevant support services, for example legal, social, medical and English language learning provision for the adults and they can encourage the children and their families to be part of the school community. They also need to be sensitive to the fact that there may not be a lot of money since most people only get £35 or so a week to spend at the supermarket so there may not be enough left over to buy the correct uniform, especially since they may have needed to move schools a few times due to changes in accommodation. Can the school help by providing uniform from spare stock?

The research report by Aspinall and Watters (2010) funded by the Equality and Human Rights Commission to examine the dimensions of equality and human rights as related to the lives of asylum seeking and refugee adults and children, notes that the policy of dispersal leads to uncertainties, disruption and a lack of continuity for the children's education. Yet it is education which can provide these children with stability and help to support their well-being. The policy of moving asylum seeking families to different areas in order to ensure that the resources in one area are not drawn on so much means that the children cannot assume that the first school they enter will be the school they are in the following year or month. The research report notes that schools with places have to admit asylum seeking and refugee children but that this is thwarted by some schools that are not prepared to receive these pupils and others that do not want the admission of these pupils to affect their GCSE results. The report highlights the fact that in one London borough there were 189 children waiting for a school place and 125 of them were asylum seekers.

The report further outlines barriers such as lack of resources in schools and variable practice which hinders the integration and educational progress of asylum seeking and refugee children. The authors noted that varied practice in schools in the admission of asylum seeking and refugee children stemmed from the assumption that this was a homogeneous group and a lack of a nuanced understanding about the needs of different groups. The report (Aspinall and Watters, 2010) highlights research undertaken by the Refugee Council to identify how schools could establish good practice to work with asylum seeking and refugee families and their children; for example by offering extended school provision which educates the children and works more broadly with their families and the wider community; assigning a home–school/community worker who can not only be a tangible link between the school and families, but can also be involved in providing wider specialist support such as inducting families and helping them to access other support agencies; and establishing peer mentors and specific language support in classes, as well as beyond the school day such as in extended provision, or on Saturday mornings which helps other members of the family.

The right to education is a basic human right and asylum seeker and refugee children are entitled to education in the countries in which they seek refuge. In most European countries these children may be sent to centres where they are educated alongside others in a similar position and where they gain proficiency in the language of that country, but in the UK these children are integrated into main-stream provision. What do you see as the advantages or disadvantages of these two approaches?

## Schools and teachers supporting the needs of asylum seeking and refugee children and their families

It is important that schools do not see refugee and asylum seeking children as a homogeneous group. They come from a variety of countries for a variety of reasons, as described above. The DfES (2004b: 4) guidance notes that children from the same country may not come from the 'same ethnic or linguistic backgrounds and their families may have different religious beliefs and political observances'. Teachers and schools should also note that children from asylum seeking and refugee backgrounds will have very different experiences of persecution in their countries of origin and their journeys to the country of refuge and varied experiences of being in that country. It is important to note that children will vary in how well they cope with the stresses associated with the change in their lives. In fact many refugees have shown how resilient they can be – an outcome which Anderson (2004) describes as something which emerges from adversity rather than a quality a person possesses or not.

Hamilton and Moore (2004) provide a developmental model which can track the changes refugee children have gone through during the sudden changes in their lives which require adaptation and resilience. Teachers need to become familiar with it as a means of recognizing the factors which may have shaped the lives of these children. The model delineates factors associated with the three stages of transition in the lives of refugee children and the associated tensions resulting from unusual and aberrant life-changing events or conditions. The stages and factors are:

1 **pre-migration factors** – experiencing the events of war or conflict such as bombing or shooting and as a consequence seeing dead and injured people; experiencing the death of or injury to a member of their family, or being injured themselves, witnessing the violent death of a family member through torture; experiencing fear, trauma and panic themselves, but also in other trusted adults; being a child soldier; disruption to their everyday routines like going to school;

2 **trans-migration factors** – suffering the anxiety and tension involved in a long and dangerous journey to escape; experiencing transition through several countries; experiencing life in a refugee camp; being at risk of exploitation and then trying to settle in different countries; the separation from parents or other loved ones;

3 **post-migration factors** – stress amongst children and adults; experiencing anxiety of whether they will be allowed to settle or not; the whole process of application; fear of deportation; the sense of loss of status and dependency on others when once the family were perhaps independent, requiring no support; overcrowded or poor housing; racism and the struggle to access health and schooling.

Richman (1998) states that all these factors impact on the child's well-being and affect their sense of security, self and identity. Inevitably there may be consequences in terms of the child's learning and progress in school, yet, as Richman (1998) asserts, a school's policy and its implementation can have a beneficial effect on the well-being of refugee children. Schools can help children feel safe and help them regain a sense of normality, and each factor sets the climate for learning. Local authorities and schools are obliged to provide full-time education for pupils of school age and to ensure there is no delay in providing schooling for asylum seeking and refugee children; local authorities should have policies and support services to assist asylum seeking and refugee families with, for example, admissions in the middle of a term since the conditions of war and flight from it do not conveniently coincide with the timing of school admissions. Local authorities should assist schools with access to interpreting services or access to Ethnic Minority Achievement Services (EMAS) staff who can assess the child's language proficiency in their first language, and they can then provide subsequent support for the child and the school. For children entering Early Years provision it is vital that the different services work together for the benefit of the child; for example, to ensure that health care professionals such as a health visitor are involved with the family and can provide them with support. Some local authorities have a designated person whose responsibility involves the welfare and education of asylum seeking and refugee children.

A good school will have induction procedures for the parents and children from asylum seeking and refugee backgrounds. The induction process will need to involve initial parental orientation and expectations of schools since schools in the UK differ from perhaps the formal schooling structures of other countries. A well thought out and patient approach to the induction process can provide these families with a sense of security and the beginnings of a trusting relationship can be established between the school and the family. It is advisable for the school staff to undertake some initial research into the conditions within the home country; the communities, languages and history of the country and some research on the schooling in that country. The information gathering process is an important stage for the school and the family but they may not want to recount the tensions that caused them to flee their country of origin. The DfES (2004b) guidance states,

> Specifically, these children need provision that can: meet their psychological needs, by, for example, using play to help a child settle; respond to their language needs; challenge racism and promote an understanding and positive acceptance of cultural diversity; involve parents who may not be confident in speaking English; support families who may be experiencing stress and economic deprivation; address issues of religious belief. (DFES, 2004b: 6)

Schools and teachers need to be aware of the language and the emotional and physical needs of asylum seeker and refugee children. In order to understand these there needs to be staff in-service training which covers such areas as finding out the child's home language, encouraging the maintenance of their home language, deploying the use of bilingual assistants, trying to learn a few key words of the child's home language such as hello and good-bye, for young children knowing the child's words for toilet or hungry or thirsty, having dual language signs and books in the classroom, involving the child in teaching the children in their class words from their home language, providing the child with good language role models who can also be their friends and be supportive – they do not have to be the same ethnicity as the asylum seeking or refugee child, but should be a trustworthy, kind and helpful buddy who can show them the routines of the school and with the teacher's help they can encourage the child to use greetings in English as a start to their development of English. For young children and their families play can provide a welcome return to normality and a means for parents and children being together through a normal childhood activity such as play. It can also help some children as a conduit to talk about their fears and hopes and in this way be therapeutic in helping them cope with the stresses they have endured. The last thing that an asylum seeking or refugee child needs to experience is isolation at school. To be alone in a strange school, in a strange country and not speak the language would instil fear into any person, adult or child; but for these children it would add to the stress and fear they have already experienced as a result of their transit to the UK. This is why schools need to be sensitive to the needs of the child and their family.

 **Case study**

Grace has just started at your school with her brother. She is 14 and has come to join her father but her mother is still in Zimbabwe. They are an asylum seeking family. Grace starts school in the middle of the Spring term just after half-term. How will her start mid-term affect her work and how can her teacher and the school support Grace to achieve her best. She is keen to become a doctor.

 **Questions for discussion**

As her form tutor what do you need to know about Grace?
What research do you need to undertake?
How will you welcome Grace into your classroom?

What is interesting about this case study is that it can be tempting to think that children from asylum seeker or refugee backgrounds are from deprived or poorly educated backgrounds. It is correct to think that the children's education may have been disrupted, but, as we can see it is not necessarily the case that all children from these two groups come from backgrounds where they either have not been to school or that they have received minimal education in their country of origin. It is right to consider the child's educational background alongside key facts such as the child's level of language proficiency in their first language; the level of education in their home country and the education or the employment of the parents in their home country. Aspinall and Watters (2010: 42) cite research which found that Somali children perform 22% below the average mean. Rutter (2006) notes that whilst Somali children's performance is below the mean in two local authorities her research found that where schools worked closely with the Somali community the children in those schools outperformed the White students but were still 11% below the national average. There was significant underachievement amongst children from the Congo which Rutter (2006) surmised was due to the 'fragility' of their first language which then in turn impeded the acquisition of English and their subsequent attainment. She found that a relatively new group of refugees from Southern Sudan performed well in school and identified factors such as family status in their home country, level of schooling and education and the fact that English was spoken at home as supportive to their educational success. Her findings showed that where the schools merely worked on homogenized conceptions about asylum seeker and refugee children and failed to recognize the specific needs of the child, that children did not achieve as well.

The duty of schools to promote community cohesion (DCSF, 2007a) should provide schools with a greater impetus to engage and liaise in tangible ways with all the communities it serves. The duty encompasses a number of other statutory requirements, such as the need to promote the children's spiritual, moral, social and cultural education (Education Act 2002) and the duty to promote race equality (Race Relations Amendment Act 2000). The duty to promote community cohesion is designed to be inclusive and to enable schools to prepare children to live in a globally diverse world but also to enable them to appreciate and live in a culturally, ethnically and religiously diverse British society. The duty is a positive attempt to help children wherever they live to value members of their school community, their local community and the global community.

This chapter has explored the distinctions between refugees and asylum seekers and how the experience of flight from their home country and the transition from one country to another can affect children's well-being, their education and their achievement. The chapter highlighted links to the International Convention on Refugees and demonstrated how this can manifest itself in the provision of education for asylum seeking and refugee children. But most importantly, the reader was encouraged to develop a nuanced concept of the children that are part of this group and to begin to understand that their individual stories will illuminate their fears, hopes and needs. Teachers and education professionals need to take time to understand the whole story to meet the needs of the individual child.

## Further reading

- Laird, E. (2007) *Kiss the Dust*. London: Macmillan Children's Books.
- Zephaniah, B. (2001) *Refugee Boy*. London: Bloomsbury.

## Useful websites

- Equality and Human Rights Commission: www.equalityhumanrights.com
  - o Promotes equality and human rights; aims to create a fairer Britain by providing advice and guidance, and raising awareness of people's rights
- Multiverse: www.multiverse.ac.uk
  - o A website for teacher educators and student teachers addressing the educational achievement of pupils from diverse backgrounds
- Refugee Council Online: www.refugeecouncil.org.uk
  - o The largest organization in the UK working with asylum seekers and refugees offering direct help and support
- Scottish Refugee Council: www.scottishrefugeecouncil.org.uk
  - o Independent charity dedicated to providing advice, information and assistance to asylum seekers and refugees living in Scotland
- Shared Futures: www.sharedfutures.org.uk
  - o A DVD and resource pack that promotes the integration of refugee children and young people in school and the wider community
- Teachers TV: www.teachers.tv
  - o A website with engaging videos, practical resources and an active online community to encourage teacher development
- UN Refugee Agency: www.unhcr.org
  - o Its primary purpose is to safeguard the rights and well-being of refugees. It strives to ensure that everyone can exercise the right to seek asylum and find safe refuge in another state, with the option to return home voluntarily, integrate locally or to resettle in a third country

# Looked-after Children – Children in Care

## Gianna Knowles

---

**This chapter explores:**

- What is meant by 'looked-after' and Children in Care (CiC);
- Why children become looked-after or need to be Children in Care;
- Children and loss;
- CiC and achievement at school;
- Resilience.

---

Children in children's homes reported being more likely than most to be threatened or to have their property taken or damaged. Children in residential special schools reported being more likely than most to be hit or hurt, to be threatened, to be treated unfairly, and to have unpleasant mobile or computer messages sent to them. Fifty six per cent of those in residential special schools reported being hit or hurt, compared with 39% for all children (Ofsted, 2008a: 16).

## Children in care

The DCSF document *Improving the Educational Attainment of Children in Care* (2009h) states as an estimate that there are currently around 60,000 Children in Care (CiC). Sixty-three per cent of the children who are taken into care have become CiC because of abuse and neglect (DCSF, 2009h: 2). Children are also taken into care because their family may be experiencing a time of severe stress, because a parent may be – or have become – disabled or because of the death of a parent. Many children who become CiC will be suffering loss, trauma and mental health problems (DCSF, 2009h: 2) and while the state has deemed that the child be taken into care for its own 'protection and wellbeing' (2009h: 2) the child themselves may still be very loyal to their family – whatever problems there have been – and may, alongside feelings of loss and abandonment, also be dealing with feelings of guilt, believing they have caused this situation or have abandoned siblings. Children also become CiC because they are refugee or asylum seekers and may be suffering trauma due to their experiences in the country they have come from and their experience of the refugee/asylum process here. This is explored in more detail in Chapter 8.

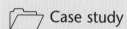 Case study

Izzy lives in the Midlands, she is 10 and has a sister two years younger. She and her sister became CiC due to family breakdown. The girls spent two years living with a foster family, they had regular contact with their mother and their mother was given support to help her deal with the challenges that were overwhelming her at the time. Once things were more stable for the family, Izzy and her sister went back to live with their mother.

Izzy says: 'My mum and dad split up, they rowed a lot first and then one day dad just wasn't there any more. I didn't miss the rows, but I did miss him. My mum found it really hard to cope, she started to drink all the time. My auntie tried to help look after us, we went to her house and she fed us and stuff, sometimes we slept there, but for a while it got really bad. Mum wasn't able to tidy up and clean the house, we didn't have clothes for school and sometimes she would forget to buy food. When we were fostered at first we were really upset, and wanted to be with our mum. We were worried about her and what was happening to her. But our foster family were very kind and it was really kind of nice to have things sort of normal and sorted out. It was hard, very hard, but now we are all back together and mum is much better.'

 Questions for discussion

Do you have any experience of being in care?
How does Izzy's experience compare with yours?
If you have been in care, what advice would you want to give to those working in schools about how best to support Izzy and her sister?

> If you have no experience of the care system make a list of things you want to know about providing for CiC. If this chapter does not address all of them, the further reading and websites at the end of the chapter might help.

## Attachment disorders

In Chapter 3 we explored how, in order to thrive and flourish, children need a home life, however diverse that might be, that will enable them to form positive bonds with caregivers. For many CiC the opportunity for developing these attachment bonds in a way that will ensure the child can thrive may be disrupted or not immediately possible to achieve. As a result, some CiC will experience attachment disorders. Prior (2006), in exploring attachment disorders, divides them into two distinct types: Disinhibited Attachment Disorder and Reactive Attachment Disorder.

### Disinhibited Attachment Disorder

A child who might be said to be manifesting symptoms of a Disinhibited Attachment Disorder (DAD) may seem unable to be selective about whom to form bonds or attachments with. In young children, who may not have had the opportunity to form secure attachments with positively responsive caregivers, the child may be indiscriminate in who they seek to form attachments with.

Where the attachment process develops in an appropriate way the young child will attach to a few primary caregivers and both child and caregiver learn to be responsive to each other. However the child with DAD may seek to form a bond with anyone who will respond and may be unselective about the responses the putative caregivers make. That is to say *any attention is better than no attention*. In this way the child may be vulnerable in that they seek attachments with those that may be shown to be abusive. The putative caregiver may not wish to bond with the child appropriately or they may be unable to respond with the appropriate care the child needs, and this may result in physical or emotional neglect. In some instances the putative caregiver may be more systematically physically or sexually abusive. Research that explores 'grooming' by paedophiles seeking a sexual relationship with a child shows that abusers will seek out children who are vulnerable in this way, children who may, because of other things happening in their lives, be displaying behaviours that include over- and indiscriminate familiarity with relative strangers (Knowles, 2009; NSPCC, 2010; Prior, 2006: 185).

Children with DAD may, for similar reasons, be unable to form secure friendship bonds with other children, they may seem to skip between friends or friendship groups. This can cause other children to reject the child as they become wary of the child's inconsistent behaviour, particularly if the child discloses 'secrets' to other 'friends' or friendship groups that they had been told in confidence. Children with DAD may also show other signs of 'emotional or behavioural disturbance' (Prior, 2006: 185), by behaving in ways not expected for a child of their age or at odds with their peer group.

### Reactive Attachment Disorder

While the child who is showing behaviours consistent with DAD may be indiscriminate in seeking attachment with others, a child with Reactive Attachment Disorder (RAD) will often fail to 'respond in a developmentally appropriate way to most social interactions' (Prior, 2006: 185). For example they may seem very watchful or avoid or resist comforting by others. They may seem unmoved by greetings or partings or others' signs of distress. They may show signs of extreme misery, be fearful, aggressive or unresponsive (Prior, 2006: 185). A child who shows signs of RAD may be one who has experienced abuse or neglect from caregivers. However, abuse does not always result in RAD.

## Attachment and being a CiC

The age of a child placed in care and where they are placed will also have a bearing on the child's experience of attachment. For example, if a child is placed in a home, where there are a number of children needing particular attention, the quality of care is different to that which might, ideally, be offered by a foster family. In an institution it may not be appropriate for staff to allow children to become strongly attached to any one person, in the main to protect the child who may be moving on to another placement or the staff may themselves leave. Such institutions may in all other respects provide excellent care for the child, but be unable to provide children with the secure attachment experiences they need. Similarly, those working in schools may be sought out by children seeking a secure attachment with a caregiver and this is picked up later in the chapter.

We also explored in Chapter 3 how the work of Bronfenbrenner developed the concept of the interrelatedness of children's growth and their experience of society and different social groups. A child who is placed in a children's home or care institution for any length of time, including where a child is an asylum seeker or refugee child, will have a more restricted microsystem and mesosystem. It may also be that because their pool of adults and significant others that they come into contact with may be more restricted than that of other children, this may limit or distort how ideas and events are conveyed to them from the wider social sphere of the exosystem. Research shows that children who can be placed in foster care, with adoptive families or returned to their biological families, including grandparents or aunts and uncles, if it is not possible for the child to be returned to their parents, before the age of seven, are more likely to thrive in a way comparable with children who have not been CiC (Prior, 2006).

 **Activity**

Thinking about schools you have worked in, or the school you currently work in, are you aware of:

- The school's policy for meeting the needs of CiC?
- Any training the school offers about the particular needs of CiC?
- Who to talk to about working with a CiC?

## Being in care and feelings of loss

The children you work with who are CiC may have only recently been placed in care, or they may have been in care for a number of years. Even children who have only been in care for a short while may already have been moved a number of times. For children who have been in care for a while, they may have had stayed in more than one children's home or with more than one foster family. For some children who are CiC, as well as dealing with the care situations they may be coming to terms with feelings of loss. Loss is the term used to describe the emotional and sometimes physical traumatic reaction some children go through when someone or something of great psychological importance to them is lost – and for children in care this may be their home and their family. Children experience loss because families collapse, parents and caregivers separate or divorce, and in very severe cases of loss, parents and caregivers die. As we have also seen in Chapter 8 CiC may be suffering loss because of war situations they have experienced in their own country or from having to flee their home. That is, CiC are in care because they have lost their caregivers either through death, or through other potentially traumatic events.

Loss can be particularly traumatic for children because as developing human beings they may not yet have the mature coping mechanisms in place to help them deal with the shock of the loss and the strength of the feelings it produces. They also do not have the life experience to be able to begin to contextualize why things have happened and the likelihood of them happening again – feelings which can be compounded if the child has also been moved a number of times while in care. Di Ciacco (2008) suggests that:

> A significant loss can incur a deep psychological wound that sharply alters the child's worldview and requires intervention to adjust that child's expectations about life, to give her coping skills for future disappointments and to avoid missteps. With a trauma, a child unconsciously builds an invisible wall to hide her pain and shut out terror. (Di Ciacco, 2008: 24)

Therefore, as someone supporting a child who is a CiC, it is helpful to be aware of some of the signs of 'loss' that children might be exhibiting.

---

### Possible indicators that a child is coming to terms with feelings of loss

One indicator that a child is experiencing feelings of loss is that they may exhibit **shock** and **numbness**.

The child may also show signs of **denial**. They may behave as if nothing in their lives is different. This is a normal part of the process of dealing with loss. For example, the child who is experiencing loss may explain that their parent is 'away on holiday' or 'staying with their friend' which is why they are being looked after by someone else.

The child may understand the facts about the loss but be **unable to comprehend** what the wider implications of that might mean. They may also deny that the change to their daily living arrangements means that other daily routines might need to change. In this way the child may be trying to make some sense of what is happening to them, by trying to keep things as before. Often children can be helped to deal with this aspect of loss by explaining to them what will happen next, *who will do what, when, where and how* (Chara, 2005; Di Ciacco, 2008: 52; Knowles, 2010).

Again depending on how old the child is and their maturity and experience, they may be feeling emotions they have never felt before and be unable to name. Therefore, children may need support in dealing with the **unfamiliar emotions** caused by their loss or changes to the situation they are now living in.

---

Many who work with children in schools know children who have suffered or are suffering loss, perhaps because of family breakdown or through being a CiC. However, without some specific training or guidance in this area it can be very hard to know how to help children dealing with loss. In particular, children who are bereaved because of the death of a parent may require specialist support in helping them come to terms with their loss. If you want to know more about supporting children in dealing with feelings of loss, particularly if they are bereaved, you may find some of the suggested further readings and websites listed at the end of the chapter helpful. It might also be helpful to you and those you work with to suggest that some training to help children deal with loss might be useful.

Thinking about children suffering loss may be challenging for you, perhaps because it brings up memories of things that have happened in your own life. Or you may feel helpless in terms of knowing how to support a child. If you have your own memories you are finding it challenging to deal with, it may help you to seek some support for yourself. When you are working with children, your first priority is them, so you will be better placed to support them if you are feeling strong yourself.

## Adoption

In the context of the ideas we have just been exploring it is also important to consider children who have been adopted as many children who are adopted do, at some point in their lives, experience feelings of loss, and many children are adopted from having been a CiC. For many children who are adopted being 'an adopted child' will occasion more challenges than those experienced as part of the general challenges of growing up.

Often a child who is adopted will go through a period of needing to grieve for the loss of their birthmother and birth family. Where a child was adopted at a very young age and has a 'usual' parent–child relationship with their adoptive parents their feelings may also be compounded by feeling guilty about loving the parents they are with but also missing their birthmother. Children do not always have the words or experience to explain how they are feeling. A child who has been adopted at a very young age may have been told their 'adoption story' and may often repeat it in what seems to be a very matter of fact way. However, this apparent clarity in the telling of the story may mask very strong feelings a child has about what actually happened. For example, they may have feelings about having 'lost' their birthmother or having been rejected and abandoned by their birthmother. These feelings may intensify as the child gets older and begins to understand the wider implications of what it means to be adopted. Similarly the situation may be compounded where the child has been adopted from a birth culture or country different to that they are now living in.

There is considerable support available to both adopted children and adoptive families, and the grief and loss experienced by adopted children is well documented. It is now understood, particularly in terms of identity development, how important it is to enable a child to have contact with their birth culture or country, where they have been adopted into another culture or removed from the country they were born in. There is also support available to children for when and if they want to make contact with their birthmother. For a child who has spent some time in care before being adopted their feelings may be even more confused. Again, helping children deal with these situations may require specialist help and support, for both the child and the school. Similarly it is not possible to cover here everything that might help you support children in these situations. What is important, however, is that by engaging with this material you are raising your own awareness of what children may be experiencing and how these experiences may be impacting on their achievement and learning. Thinking about these situations will also make you more proactive in wanting to find out how best to support these children; make enquiries what training might be available and to be assertive in ensuring your school has the correct policies and practices in place for supporting children dealing with what may be challenging times in their lives.

## The impact of being a CiC on the child's ability to achieve in school

This chapter has explored what it means when we say a child is a CiC, in the legal terms of what that means, the diversity of the care situations a child might be placed in and in the diverse experiences of care children will have. The chapter has also explored how being a CiC may impact on the emotional well-being of the child. This section of the chapter now considers how being a CiC can impact on children in terms of their educational achievement. In 2009 the Department for Children, Schools and Families published *Improving the Educational Attainment of Children in Care (Looked after Children)*. In part the publication was in response to its findings that: 'In 2008, just 14% of children in care achieved 5, A*–C grade GCSEs' (DCSF, 2009h: 2), where the expected average is that 50.7% of children should be achieving, A*–C grade GCSEs (DCSF, 2010a). It was the DCSF's concern that CiC are failing to achieve as they should, and in line with their peer group.

The child's experience of the care system, particularly if they have been moved to and from a number of placements, will impact on their engagement with school. The DCSF's findings (2009h) also show that some of the barriers to achievement CiC encounter at school are because:

> the school system itself doesn't do enough to help looked after children catch up and keep up – either because schools don't know that children are in care or because they do not know what can be done to accelerate their learning. (DCSF, 2009h: 1)

While being a CiC may address a child's immediate needs for a home and care the concern is that CiC do not seem to be thriving at school. Not only are CiC moved from school to school more often than others in their peer group, but research also shows that a higher proportion of CiC are deemed to have an SEN as compared with other members of their peer group: 28%, where as the average is 3% (DCSF, 2009h). Lack of educational achievement in the primary phase can have a cumulative effect, such that when children who have been CiC leave school a higher proportion of them, compared to the rest of their peer group, will leave at 16 and 'they are less than half as likely to end up in education, employment or training as their peers and there is a disproportionate probability that they will be teenage parents' (DCSF, 2009h: 2). Research also shows that 'children in care who have been moved frequently from placement to placement are nearly three times more likely to be detained in a youth offending institution or prison' (www.communitycare.co.uk).

---

### Removing barriers to the achievement of CiC – ensuring equal access to achievement in school

In response to the concern for the lack of achievement experienced by CiC the DCSF recommended that putting some or all of the following procedures in place, will enable a school to better support their CiC:

- Admissions procedures should prioritize CiC to ensure they have access to the schools best suited to meet their needs;
- Movement between schools should be kept to an absolute minimum;
- Personalized learning is ensured for all CiC and it will be supported by a Personal Education Allowance of £500;
- Each school is required, by law, to provide a designated teacher who supports the learning of CiC and is aware of the particular needs of CiC;
- The school's leadership team ensure a school ethos of inclusive support for CiC. (DCSF, 2009h)

Activity

Below is a checklist that indicates what to look for in terms of the role of the designated teacher and personalized learning for CiC. When you next have the opportunity to be in a school use the checklist to find out what provision is being made for CiC.

The designated teacher is responsible for ensuring that each CiC has a **Personal Education Plan (PEP)**, this will include noting any particular needs the child has and strategies that will support the child's learning.

The £500 Personal Educational Allowance can be used to provide any additional activities the child might benefit from: after school activities, books and other resources, trips – to the theatre, for example – that might usually be provided by parents.

The PEP might also stipulate that a strategy the child might benefit from is one-to-one tuition. The child should be involved in the drawing up and regular reviews of their PEP.

The designated teacher is responsible for ensuring educational opportunities are created for the child which will provide them with equality of access to learning to enable them to achieve in ways comparable to other children in their peer group. They are responsible for understanding the wider needs of the child – that is, to be aware of the opportunities the child may not have access to, because they are a CiC.

The designated teacher is also responsible for ensuring the child's social worker and carers are involved in the PEP.

Ideas to consider:

If you are working with CiC, or are interested to know how best to support CiC, talk to the teacher designated to support the CiC. Ask them about the school's policy for supporting CiC and how some of the children have been using their Personal Education Allowance.

## Examples of good practice in supporting CiC

In 2010 the then QCDA provided the following good examples of how a Midlands town works with CiC to help support their achievement at school.

### Relationships with school staff and feelings about school

Every six weeks the children who are part of the scheme work with education staff to discuss Pupil Attitudes to Self and School (PASS). Through talking, the adult and child can explore what is going well at school and what's a challenge, particularly how they are feeling about school and how they feel the adults in the school are responding to them. For children who are not in care or looked after, these are the sorts of conversations they might have with adults at home, but for a child in care there may not be that opportunity or they may need to learn that everyone can find school challenging and gets on with some adults and not others. The atmosphere is informal as again the child may not have the life experience or another opportunity to put adults in school in a context other than being 'authority' figures. The QCDA material states that: 'as a result, their relationships improve, they feel valued and are positive about being back in learning' (QCDA 2010b).

### Continuity support

The local authority also provides a 'team of teachers and learning mentors who support children, schools, carers and social workers' (QCDA, 2010b) to support the children and the schools. Some of the team are attached to the residential homes some of the children may be living in and, again, in this way can provide continuity for the child between 'home' and school.

### Personalizing the curriculum

It is recognized that in order to support the children to achieve, providing equality of access to learning for them will mean ensuring their learning is personalized in a way that is appropriate for their needs – which for these CiC included: 'Summer in the city' which provided children in foster care with the opportunity to 'try arts activities, music and dance, outdoor pursuits, canoeing, climbing, skiing, rollerblading and swimming' (QCDA, 2010b).

## Teachers as significant others

In this, and previous chapters, we have discussed how important 'others' are in the lives of children. We have explored how part of the opportunities children need, particularly in terms of the diversity of the backgrounds they can come from, are the opportunities to build positive and respectful relationships with adults they can trust. We have seen how having these relationships allow children to flourish and thrive and achieve in their learning. For many children, including CiC, part of the contribution to enabling them to achieve in their learning that you make, will be in modelling what a secure and trusting relationship should be like. Since between the ages of five and 16, 'children in the UK spend most of their waking hours in formal education' (Foley et al., 2001: 20).

Schools are generally very consistent, safe, ordered places with well-structured days, routines and regulations which are generally appropriately enforced. While this can sometimes seem quite limiting, in many ways it is the role of schools to perform these functions. For CiC who may have experienced very chaotic lives, the structure of the school day can be both liberating and confining. It is part of normal child development for children to 'test' those who are looking after them and, for a CiC, you may be one of a number of adults who fall into that category. Testing caregivers serves two functions: firstly such testing is often the child, unconsciously, testing the caregiver to see if they will still love them unconditionally, even though they have been 'naughty', and secondly, the child will 'test boundaries' to see how far they can go with particular behaviours before they are sanctioned. If children do not learn about boundaries they can make themselves vulnerable, or abuse others – through violent behaviour and bullying, for example. In the usual course of events, children learn to regulate themselves and their behaviours through interaction with parents and other family members, but for a CiC, depending on where they are placed and their life experiences, teachers and other adults in school may be those who the child is testing their behaviour against. While a child may seem to be rebelling against the routines and rules of the school, they are actually testing boundaries and need to know that there are boundaries and this is what makes school a secure and safe place and teachers and other adults people who can be trusted (Waterman, 2003).

Depending on what a CiC has experienced their behaviour may be very testing for the school, as Waterman (2003) states: '... the child has to have enough opportunity to ruthlessly use the parent (or therapist [or adult in school]) for his own emotional purposes (as an extension of self) without any regard for the parent's needs or individuality' (Waterman, 2003: 133). Only when a child has been through this phase – which in the normal course of events will happen between the ages of two and seven, depending on when the child has had the opportunity to undergo this developmental process – will the child be *emotionally and cognitively* ready to take on the responsibility for managing their own actions and for their actions towards others. For CiC this process may be delayed because there has not yet been a safe enough place for the development to take place.

## Resilience

Many of the issues explored in this book serve to highlight just how diverse the lives of even very young children can be. It can be tempting to want to romanticize childhood and think of it as a charmed time of innocence and joy, and this view of childhood is one that is supported by many dominant discourses in society. Many children do enjoy a childhood as loved and cherished children, however, most families and children will experience some life events that will be a testing time for them and their families. Schools have both a legal and moral responsibility to recognize the diverse life experiences children have and to work with children and often their families to support them through these events. It is not possible to 'fix' some of the issues children have to deal with, but what has been shown is that where children are supported through the challenges they are facing, whether, in this instance, that is being taken into care or suffering some form of loss, children will find the resources to deal with the situation and move on. This capacity to adjust to and survive such challenges is known as *resilience* – 'the ability to rebound from crisis and overcome life challenges' (Walsh, 2006: ix). Resilience is not necessarily something some children seem to have been born with and others not, resilience, just as any capacity we have, can be developed and strengthened. Resilience is developed through acknowledging that there is adversity and finding ways of dealing with it. It might not be possible in the short-term to 'solve' the problem that is causing the adversity, but by finding strategies for addressing the aspects of it that can be dealt with, the child can be enabled to have some control over some of what is happening to them. This will also make the problem seem less like a chaotic mess about which the child can do nothing. As Walsh (2006) discusses, resilience is developed through working effectively through difficulties, both in terms of dealing with our own reactions and feelings to them and through taking control of those things we can do something about or solving some of the problems. Resilience is about integrating 'the fullness of a crisis experience into the fabric of our individual and collective identity, influencing how we go on to live our lives' (Walsh, 2006: 6).

In the examples of good practice cited earlier in the chapter that discuss how CiC or children dealing with loss have been helped, the most important factor was having a designated adult to support them. The role of this adult is both to meet with them regularly and to listen to how the child is really experiencing things; to discuss what might be going well and what is still challenging. It is the role of this adult to hear what the child is saying and act as the child's advocate to 'get things done' for the child. The designated adult – or advocate – is the link between the child and the wider workings of the school and society. Depending on what the needs of the child might be, the designated adult can liaise with others in the school or outside agencies to gain more direct support. Again, as Walsh explores: 'with supportive relationships, training, and practice, we can strengthen resilience' (Walsh, 2006: 7), in this way we can enable children to 'deal better with traumatic events and life challenges' (2006: 7). For example, the designated adult may, after having had one of their regular reviews – or 'check-in chats' – with the child need to then explore with a colleague that the child is anxious because they have been repeatedly told off for being late, explaining that this is a temporary situation since, because of what is currently happening in the child's life they are living with their grandmother who lives quite a distance from the school. Indeed the school is very supportive of the grandmother for taking on this responsibility, since she is working with the school to ensure the child continues to attend, providing the child with continuity as well as care. In this way the designated adult can enable the child to develop resilience by seeing that some aspects of the problem can be solved, particularly internal tensions in the school, and can ensure that, for example, the child has the necessary resources and access to materials to complete homework – including somewhere to do the work.

---

### What children say about being in care

In 2009 on behalf of the Children's Rights Director for England, Ofsted published *Care and Prejudice: A Report of Children's Experience.* The report outlines the responses of 316 children surveyed about their experiences of being in care.

In the report there are examples of children talking about their feelings of loss, particularly in terms of missing their brothers and sisters. However, the report also gives many examples about what worked well for them, in terms of being in care. The children said that what had been positive about the experience were things like: 'meeting new people ... having good carers or staff ... being looked after properly' and they also talked about how they enjoyed the opportunities to have days out and holidays. For some children the positives were about 'having material things of your own' and 'support' (Children's Rights Director for England, 2009: 7).

The children spoken to were also very clear about what they meant by support, which included very direct help in learning how to do things like cook and wash things – to learn how to be independent and look after themselves. It might mean including support in dealing with health problems that had been neglected and being helped with strategies to manage feelings of anger and frustration. For many children 'being in care had meant getting away from danger':

'being away from mum and dad's behaviour – having a normal life'; 'I feel happier because I am away from abuse'; 'living here I'm out of danger'; 'my dad stopped hitting us – I love my foster family'.

Being in care could mean:

'I get treated a thousand times better'; 'not being scared'; 'not getting beaten up'; and 'I have security and love' (Children's Rights Director for England, 2009: 7).

## Further reading

- Baker, L. and Credland, S. (ed.) (2004) *Listen Up: The Voices of Homeless Children.* London: Shelter.
- Cameron, R. J. and Maginn, C. (2009) *Achieving Positive Outcomes for Children in Care.* London: Sage.
- Chara, K.A. (2005) *A Safe Place for Caleb: An Interactive Book for Kids, Teens and Adults with Issues of Attachment, Grief, Loss, or Early Trauma.* London: Jessica Kingsley Publishers.
- Knowles, G. (ed.) (2010) *Supporting Inclusive Practice,* 2nd edn. Abingdon: Routledge. See particularly Chapter 7 which deals with children coming to terms with loss and bereavement.
- Ofsted (2008) *Children's Care Monitor 2008: Children's Views on How Care is Doing: A Report by the Children's Rights Director.* London: Ofsted.
- Walsh, F. (2006) *Strengthening Family Resilience.* New York: The Guilford Press.

## Useful websites

- Winston's Wish: www.winstonswish.org.uk
  - o Leading childhood bereavement charity and the largest provider of services to bereaved children, young people and their families in the UK
- National Society for the Prevention of Cruelty to Children: www.nspcc.org.uk
  - o Leading UK child protection charity who offer advice, support, consultancy and much more
- Childline: www.childline.org.uk
  - o A UK-based counselling service for children and young people

# 10

# Enabling Equality and Achievement for Children with Disability

## Gianna Knowles

---

**This chapter explores:**

- Disability and the law in Britain;
- What 'being disabled' means;
- Barriers to learning for disabled children, including how the prevalence of bullying of disabled children impacts on well-being and achievement;
- What constitutes good practice in providing for disabled children and their families;
- Supporting equality of opportunity and the achievement of  disabled children.

---

The poverty, disadvantage and social exclusion experienced by many disabled people is not the inevitable result of their impairments or medical conditions, but rather stems from attitudinal and environmental barriers ... it is social 'barriers' which cause 'disability' not impairments or medical conditions ... These barriers can be:

- prejudice and stereotypes
- the way things are organised and run
- the way things are designed, such as little or no access to information, buildings and transport. (Ofsted, 2008b: 13–14)

In terms of equality of opportunity, disabled children are amongst the most marginalized and underachieving children in mainstream schools

(Stobbs, 2008). The Disability and Discrimination Act 1995 (DDA) and the subsequent Special Educational Needs and Disability Act 2001 have meant that since 2002: 'it has been unlawful to discriminate against disabled children and young people in the provision of any service' (Stobbs, 2008: 8). While some of the legislation in these acts requires different things from different providers, in terms of schools' provision there are two main duties under the DDA which schools have a legal duty to comply with. Schools must not treat disabled children 'less favourably' than other children and that they must make 'reasonable adjustments' to enable disabled children to attend school and enjoy and achieve at school (Stobbs, 2008: 9). While many schools responded well to the DDA and made reasonable adjustments to their provision to enable disabled children to attend school, some schools stated that the adjustments they would have to make to meet the needs of disabled children that wanted to attend their school were unreasonable. That is, they claimed that the adjustments they would have to make could not reasonably be made, in terms of the cost to the school and the expertise the school could offer a disabled child, and also that the child would not reasonably be able to get to the school or move around the school because of the nature of the premises once there. In 2005 the DDA was further strengthened by bringing in the 'disability equality duty for all "public authorities"' (Stobbs, 2008: 9). The disability equality duty (DED) requires that all public authorities, including schools, rather than responding to issues relating to disability as they happen, become proactive in putting into place policies and actions that will ensure disabled children have an equal opportunity to achieve alongside able-bodied children. Therefore, while previously a school might have felt that the adjustments it would have to make to its provision to accept a disabled child would be beyond that which might be deemed 'reasonable', now all schools must ensure that they are actively seeking to ensure that they are in a position to provide for the needs of a disabled child who may wish to attend the school (Disability Rights Commission, 2010a).

 Activity

The principles underpinning the DED are that it should actively promote equal opportunities for disabled children. This means schools need to think ahead to prepare and plan for disabled children's needs, rather than reactively trying to put something in place when a child with a disability wants to come to the school.

Schools must ensure that there is no unlawful discrimination in the school, as defined by the DDA. This may mean that all adults who work in the school would benefit from additional professional development to ensure they are up-to-date with the recent legislation and can engender a culture that supports the achievement of children with disabilities in the school. As we have seen, proving equality of opportunity is about something more that ensuring everyone has 'the same'. Indeed, under the DED schools should be actively promoting positive attitudes towards disabled children and adults and ensuring children are not bullied because of their disability.

Schools should also be proactive in seeking to meet the needs of disabled children even if this means the disabled children in the school are being more favourably treated than the able-bodied children in the school (Disability Rights Commission, 2010a).

When you are next in a school and have the opportunity:

- Read the school's polices that deal directly with meeting the needs of disabled children – are there policies that deal specifically with the needs of children who are disabled, or do children with disabilities feature in a range of policies?
- How clear are you about the legislation relating to the Disability Discrimination Act? Does the school have any helpful information about it? Has there been any recent professional development for staff about children with disabilities? If not, is any planned?
- What is the school's response to the disability equality duty – is there readily available information for all adults working in the school that outlines how the school is dealing with it?
- Is the school actively promoting positive images of disability – what can you see around the school that shows it is?
- Is disability routinely discussed in lessons – through PSE lesson activities, for example?
- Is work done with parents and in the community to encourage understanding about disability?

## What does 'being disabled' mean?

The DDA says that 'a person has a disability if he or she has a physical or mental impairment, which has a substantial and long-term adverse effect on his or her ability to carry out normal day-to-day activities'. (Ofsted 2008a: 13)

The Disability Rights Commission in their *Code of Practice for Schools* (2003) define a substantial adverse effect as being 'a limitation going beyond the normal differences in ability which might exist among people' (DRC, 2005: 144). These limitations are also ones that are likely to last longer than 12 months, so, for example, an able-bodied adult or child might break their leg and have temporary mobility problems, but in the normal course of events their leg should heal and they should return to their usual mobile self within 12 months. In the same way, the notion of 'normal difference' recognizes that there are differences between children in terms of their cognitive abilities, for example, or their height, their ability to run quickly or not; however these differences usually fall into a range of what is generally expected in a child of a given age. Anything that impacts on a child's capacity to move around or manipulate objects, that impairs their physical co-ordination or ability to control bodily functions, speak, hear, see, cognition – including concentration and being able to perceive danger – may count as a disability (DRC, 2002: 145) – particularly if the child is limited in doing those normal activities which other children of the same age can undertake. However, what it is perhaps most important to bear in mind is that a child may have a physical disability but this does not mean they will therefore have a cognitive impairment. Having a physical disability does not necessarily impact on a child's ability to learn – or to want to do all the things they see other children doing (Westwood, 2007: 34).

 Case study

'My brother Nehanda is 10. When you just see him he looks fine, but he has problems with learning things, so he doesn't know about what you should behave like when you're out. He also can't talk which is why I am telling you all this. At home we know about Nehanda and what he likes, when he's happy and when he is upset. He likes it when I read books to him and tell him stories with these puppets I've got. He likes pizza and he likes to dance!'

'When I was little I used to hate going out with him as it was so embarrassing, people would stare or, if he was behaving badly, move away from him. Now I'm older I just get angry. We can't go anywhere where we have to wait for something or queue up – so we can't go to any theme parks and go on rides. We can't go out and eat in restaurants as his behaviour "upsets the other customers". It's really hard to do something like go on holiday and go somewhere really different, or even to take him swimming at the local leisure centre. It's so unfair, it's not just Nehanda it affects, it also affects my life and mum's. He's not violent or anything, he just needs people to be more open minded about what they expect from him. People at the local shops and the library, who have known him for years are OK, it's just strangers. You'd think people nowadays would know about disability and make the effort, but it's always my mum having to say "oh I'm so sorry about my son's behaviour". I won't say sorry, I just stare back.'

 Questions for discussion

If you are disabled, or have a family member who is disabled, how does this case study reflect your experiences?
How do you think society generally can be made more aware of the needs of children like Nehanda?
As someone who works with children, what do you think a school's role is in generally educating everyone about disability?

## The social model of disability

While the DDA outlines what disability means in terms of physical and sensory impairment, this model of establishing 'disability' has been criticized. Discussing disability in this way problematizes the concept of disability. This is evident from the language used to discuss disability, where terms such as 'impairment' and 'limitation' are used. In many ways it is the language of the able-bodied who have the world constructed to meet their needs and therefore view those with disabilities as being limited, because the able-bodied have built a world of stairs and narrow doors, and who only present information in ways that have to be seen or heard. The social model of disability explores the idea that 'The "problem" of disability results from social structures and attitudes, rather than from a person's impairment or medical condition' and that its aim is 'to understand and dismantle the barriers which exclude and limit the life chances of disabled people' (Disability Rights Commission, 2010b: 9)

Issues of access, either to places or information are technical problems which, compared to changing people's attitudes, are quite straightforward to address. Where the challenge lies, in ensuring children with particular physical or sensory needs are enabled to have the equality of opportunity to achieve, is more often with changing people's attitudes to enabling it to happen, as much as making 'disabled friendly' changes to the environment. As we can see from what Nehanda's sister says, it is others' values, attitudes and beliefs that are limiting the life of her brother and also her life and that of her mother.

One of the principles of the disability equality duty is that children and adults who have a sensory or physical disability are consulted and their views sought and acted upon to ensure things are effectively improved for them (Disability Rights Commission, 2010a: 8).

---

## The voice of the child with disability

As with many activities we engage children in at school, it can be very tempting to plan and organize something for children that we believe they will find motivating and interesting. It can be a very illuminating experience to talk to children about what they do actually find interesting about their learning and in what ways they think it could be even more stimulating. The current Ofsted Inspection Framework for Primary Schools requires, as part of the inspection process, that children's opinions about the school are canvassed and that inspectors write a letter to the children explaining the inspectors' findings after the inspection.

In the same way, in terms of seeking to ensure equal opportunities for children with disability, schools have often fallen into the trap of assuming they know what the children need. This may be true with regard to ensuring access to and around the school and other forms of practical support, but this is more about the disability than the child. In 2009 the National Children's Bureau published *What is the Disabled Children's Manifesto for Change?* (National Children's Bureau, 2009), where in canvassing children's views about what they wanted to be happening for them, the children and young people said:

'Give me a choice and don't assume you know what I want.'

'I get fed up because there aren't enough places to go with suitable activities for young people.' (Patrick)

'You can't get to places, like if you want to go and meet your friends in town.' (Kim)

'When they don't talk to you or talk to your parents ... it's like I'M HERE!' (Danielle) (National Children's Bureau, 2009: 5, 6)

Since the DDA and increased access to mainstream schools for children with disabilities, what many adults working with children with disabilities have found is how like 'all children', children with disabilities are. Once people have learnt to see beyond the 'problem' of the disability, they understand that children with disabilities, just like all children, can be naughty, anxious, funny, have their likes and dislikes, may not want to do maths today but do want to use the computer...

Research also shows that in schools where all children know about disability and there is a culture of respect and mutual support for all children, where it is expected that all children will be included in all activities, then all children, including children with disabilities thrive.

## The Special Educational Needs Code of Practice

The *Special Educational Needs*: *Code of Practice* (DfES, 2001) is the DfES/DCSF document used in schools to outline how schools should work with children and families with special needs, including disabilities. The SEN Code of Practice defines physical and mental impairment in the following way:

> There is a wide spectrum of sensory, multi-sensory and physical difficulties. The sensory range extends from profound and permanent deafness or visual impairment through to lesser levels of loss ... Physical impairments may arise from physical, neurological or metabolic causes that only require appropriate access to educational facilities and equipment; others may lead to more complex learning and social needs; a few children will have multi-sensory difficulties some with associated physical difficulties. (DfES, 2001: 88)

By mental impairment the document means children who have learning difficulties and or impairment resulting from, or consisting of, a mental illness. A child who has suffered severe disfigurement is also covered by the DDA since this is an impairment which will require the school to be sensitive to not only the condition the child has, but also the social and psychological challenges that the condition might occasion.

Also covered by the DDA are some medical conditions, particularly those that may change or degenerate as the child gets older, for example, muscular dystrophy. The DDA is also very specific in stating that children and adults with cancer, multiple sclerosis and HIV infection are covered by the DDA definition of disabled, as well as children and adults registered blind or partially sighted. The underlying principle of what constitutes disability is understanding that the term refers to the long-term effect on a child's ability to carry out normal everyday activities.

## Bullying

There is a range of research (DfES, 2006c; Lamb, 2009; Ofsted, 2008a) that shows that children with disabilities are more likely to be bullied than any other group of children. We know that children who suffer bullying are also likely to achieve less at school. Further to this, failing to stop bullying is failing to ensure equality of opportunity since bullied children are not experiencing school as a safe and secure environment where they can enjoy and achieve in their learning. The 2008 Ofsted report *Children's Care Monitor*

*2008: Children's Views on how Care is Doing: A Report by the Children's Rights Director* found that:

> ... children with a disability were more likely to be bullied. Twenty per cent of children with a disability were being bullied often or always, compared with 9% for all children, and 43% of children with a disability said they were never or hardly ever bullied, compared with 67% for everyone. (Ofsted, 2008a: 14)

That the bullying of children with disabilities seems to go unreported, or unnoticed or is somehow more acceptable than bullying of other children is reflected in wider society's seeming almost *acceptance* of bullying of disabled adults.

---

### Bullying and disability

In 2007 Fiona Pilkington set fire to her car killing both herself and her disabled daughter. At the inquest into the deaths the coroner and jury heard how Fiona and her son and daughter had been subjected to violence and abuse from, mainly, youths in their community. 'Ms Pilkington's son Anthony, who has severe dyslexia, was locked in a shed at knifepoint and beaten with a metal bar' (BBC, 2009b). Fiona's daughter Francecca, who had learning difficulties, was shouted at by the gang and told to 'lift up her nightdress. They also pelted the family's home with eggs, flour and stones and shouted insults about the children's disabilities'.

Although Fiona had contacted Leicestershire Police 33 times between 2000 and 2007 and had contacted them 13 times 'in the 10 months before her death ... police filed the incidents as the less serious "grade two" and considered her to be "over-reacting". (Murder mother's abuse "ignored"' BBC, 2009b)

While this might seem to be a particularly tragic and unusual case there is evidence that the BBC have been reporting that bullying of children and adults with disabilities is higher than for other members of the population since 1999 (BBC, 1999). Similarly in 1999 Mencap, the charity organization that supports the needs of those with learning difficulties, published *Living in Fear*, its research into the experiences of being disabled and being bullied (Mencap, 1999; Knowles, 2010).

---

As we have already discussed, it is often people's values, attitudes and beliefs about disability that causes those who are disabled to experience discrimination, including bullying. Where schools and able-bodied children are working with the belief that: 'students with disabilities are more like all other children than they are different from them' (Westwood, 2007: 17), disabled children are likely to experience an inclusive learning environment that meets their needs. Similarly, schools need to keep in mind that children: 'with a particular disability ... as a group are just as diverse in their personal characteristics, behaviour, interests, and learning aptitudes as any other group of students' (Westwood, 2007: 17). Sometimes, there can be the assumption that the disabled child *is* the disability; that is, that all children who, for example, have cerebral palsy, can be 'treated' as if they were a homogenous group rather than understanding that, as with all children, we are working with individuals, and individuals who each have their own identity and personality.

---

### Stopping bullying

The resource pack *Make Them Go Away* (DCSF, 2009i) outlines some helpful guidance for schools to support them in understanding and dealing with bullying of disabled children.

Bullying of this nature can, as with racism, be unwitting or institutional. The bullying experienced by disabled children may be covert through being in an environment where there are 'negative attitudes to disability'.

A child with a disability may be more prone to being bullied as they may 'find it more difficult to resist bullies or be isolated and without protective friends'. Similarly, 'they may not understand or recognise that they are bullied; have difficulty reporting bullying' or be unable to give details about the events that have happened.

Disabled children may also repeat bullying behaviours they have been subject to and 'be unaware that they are bullying others'. Disabled children may also 'find it difficult to regulate their anger and emotions' and, like many children, need support in dealing with their feelings.

(DCSF, 2009i: 8; Knowles, 2010).

---

## A checklist of good practice in working with children with disability

In most instances, again as with many children, it will be the child's parents that the school will first have contact with. Some of the things that research shows parents of disabled children are most concerned about are explored below. As you read through these concerns, you might reflect on schools you have experience of and think about when you have seen these reflected in good practice in those schools.

Parents of children with disabilities want to know that their child will be safe, particularly in terms of knowing that the school has made, or has the ability to make adjustments to ensure their child is truly included. Will their child be physically safe moving around the school, and will they be emotionally safe? Does the school and do the other children understand about disability?

 Case study

Fiona says: 'Jamie has cerebral palsy. When we were looking for pre-school provision for him because he was easy to carry around and a sweet looking, quiet boy the place we first approached said "oh yes, we'll have no problem taking him". But what people don't realize is that this is with Jamie for life, it's not like a cold, it doesn't go away after a few days. To begin with there were problems like if the key worker who did Jamie's exercises with him was ill, they wouldn't be able to take him that day. Which meant I would have to take a day off work. Or they didn't have enough experience of the condition, so they'd be on the phone saying "Mrs Reid, is it OK if Jamie does so-and-so ...? Is it OK if we let Jamie ...?". Or there were things that he could do and they wouldn't let him because they thought he couldn't. I know I sound a bit mean, but sometimes I did think "well these people are the professionals and they're asking me".'

'When we began to look around for a school for Jamie we had a much better idea of what to expect and what sorts of questions to ask. When I first met the headteacher I think she thought "we've got a right interfering mother here" and we did have some teething problems at first. I said I wanted the other children to know that Jamie had cerebral palsy and I wanted it explained to them and even the other parents if necessary. She was a bit taken aback by that, but after Jamie had been there a couple of days and the children asked questions and one of the parents was overheard telling her daughter not to play with him as "he wasn't all there" she did what we had suggested. We have a really good relationship now and because they are the professionals they say, "well we think Jamie should be learning this and trying this" and sometimes I think "oh yeah?" But they have been right and they have got more from him and expect more of him than I do sometimes. He's even been on a residential trip with them – they have been great.'

 Questions for discussion

Why do you think Jamie initially had a mixed reception at school?
What might both his preschool setting and the school have done to better prepare themselves for Jamie?
How might the children in Jamie's class have been better prepared to welcome Jamie into the school?

A key worker, or outreach worker can in such cases, prove to be a very useful support mechanism for the child, the family and the school. Having someone whose role is not to teach, but to coordinate the team and who can provide support for the child, including being able to liaise with external agencies, keeps the communication between all parties open and is a good way of ensuring equality of opportunity for the child (Stobbs, 2008: 31).

Schools receive additional funding to support children with disabilities and it can be tempting to think that all a child's needs can be met by having someone there to provide one-to-one support for them. It is rarely the case that a child needs, or benefits from, one-to-one support all the time. It may be the role of the supporting adult is to help the child become more independent and to work with the school and the other children to ensure the child with disabilities is in an inclusive environment, so that it is the environment that supports the child, not one person. 'Some children need 1:1 at particular times and some settings have clearly considered carefully how to target support at the most critical times of the school session. These times will be different according to the needs of the child' (Stobbs, 2008: 32). Where children with disabilities thrive in mainstream schools it is where there is a whole school ethos that supports them and the staff attitude is one of 'can do' (Stobbs, 2008: 33).

---

## Particular skills, particular staff

All children with disabilities will benefit from being in a school where the adults in the school have had some training about working with children with disabilities. Some of the conditions children will come to school with, will have specific requirements, that will be better supported if those working with the child have had specific training to meet those needs.

Stobbs (2008) states that in supporting children with disabilities 'there are layers of skill and expertise that contribute to the inclusion of disabled children' (Stobbs, 2008: 34). In her report for the DCSF she outlines the training and skills that will best support the child and the school.

### Generic learning support skills

These are skills that those working with the child will use all the time and are not necessarily specific to working with children with disabilities, these

*(Continued)*

*(Continued)*

are: 'observation, behaviour management, inclusive play, working with parents' (2008: 34).

Specific skills

These are skills that adults might require specific training in or knowledge of to ensure they can meet the needs of children with disabilities for example: 'alternative methods of communication, moving and handling' (2008: 34).

Individual techniques

These will be skills and knowledge needed to support the individual needs of specific children for example: 'the administration of a particular medicine, a particular method of communication or a particular feeding technique' (2008: 34).

## Multi-agency working

Since the inception of the ECM agenda, all schools have been working to develop their multi-agency practice. Multi-agency working is particularly beneficial for children with disabilities as it can:

- reduce the number of appointments and visits that families need to make;
- make for better co-ordinated provision;
- enable disabled children to join in activities with their peers; and
- act as outreach and draw children and families into provision that they might not have visited otherwise. (Stobbs, 2008: 35)

Many local authorities, particularly through their development of Children's Centres provide multi-agency support for disabled children and their families, which can also be accessed by schools to help support children to achieve in their learning. Such provision will include 'weekly drop-in play and talk sessions for under-fives' (Stobbs, 2008: 35), which can be particularly supportive for the family of a disabled child. Such centres will also provide access to 'speech and language therapists and family support workers' (Stobbs, 2008: 35). Often a centre will be able to provide specialist sessions:

> designed to promote children's play, listening, talking and social skills in a group setting and to support parents in promoting their child's communication skills through play and everyday activities. Children may be referred to the groups where there are concerns about their play or communication skills. (Stobbs, 2008: 35)

## How *The Children's Plan* seeks to support the achievement of children with disabilities

In 2007 the DCSF published its first *Children's Plan* (DCSF, 2007b) which further supports the government's realization of the Every Child Matters agenda. In terms of how children can be supported and provided with the equality of opportunity to 'enjoy and achieve' one of its central principles is that of personalized learning. The notion of personalized learning as a strategy to support the achievement of children with disabilities was introduced in the Department for Education and Skills (DfES) document *Removing Barriers to Achievement* (DFES, 2004a). The notion of how personalized learning can provide equality of opportunity for children with disabilities to achieve is outlined below.

## Personalizing learning for children with disabilities

Personalized learning is about ensuring the learning activities provided for children reflect the individual needs and interests of the child. One of its central principles is that all children can achieve in their learning and that those working with them should not lower their expectations because of the particular needs or challenging circumstances a child has. It may be the case that some careful thought will have to be given to how the child can access the learning, but knowing what interests and motivates the child will provide an entry point into the learning.

Personalized learning activities are characterised by the features given below.

- The planning of the activity is informed by discussion with the child – for example, if you want to develop particular writing genres with a child, writing a report or instructions, discuss this with the child and provide an actual experience they can write about.
- Depending on the learning intended, not all proof of learning needs to be written down. Provide a choice for pupils as to how they can present their learning – it might be possible to do it through making a model, using rap, making a poster, etc.
- Those planning learning activities worry that personalized learning will involve having to devise separate learning activities for every child in the class. This is not necessary. You need to decide what the main learning objective is about and ensure there is enough breadth in the way you have designed it that there is more than one way of demonstrating the outcome of the learning. What will then happen is that the children will self-select themselves into 'groups' who want to pursue the learning in a similar way.

The important things to keep in mind with regard to personalized learning are:

- having high expectations of all children
- building on the knowledge, interests and aptitudes of every child
- involving children in their own learning through shared objectives and feedback (assessment for learning)
- helping children to become confident learners …

Effective teaching for children with SEN including disabilities, shares most of the characteristics of effective teaching for *all* children. (DfES, 2004a: 55)

## Further reading

- DfES (2006) *Implementing the Disability Discrimination Act in Schools and Early Years Settings.* London: DfES.

- Disability Rights Commission (2002) *Code of Practice for Schools.* London: TSO.

- Disability Rights Commission (2010) *Doing the Duty: An Overview of the Disability Equality Duty for the Public Sector.* Available at: http://www.dotheduty.org/ (accessed 29.03.10).

- Disability Rights Commission (2010) *The Disability Equality Duty: Guidance on Gathering and Analysing Evidence to Inform Action.* Available at: http://www.dotheduty.org

- National Children's Bureau (2009) *What is the Disabled Children's Manifesto for Change?* Available at: www.ncb.org.uk/ (accessed 29.03.10).

- Ofsted (2008) *Ofsted Disability Equality Scheme.* London: OfSTED.

## Useful websites

- Disability Action: www.disabilityaction.org
  - o Works to ensure that people with disabilities attain their full rights as citizens by supporting inclusion, influencing government policy and changing attitudes in partnership with disabled people
- Children's Bureau: www.childrensbureau.org
  - o US-based advice and support services for adopted and fostered children and families

# Endnote

The last chapter ended with a discussion about personalized learning. While this discussion formed part of the chapter on children and disability, as with many of the ideas covered in this book, the ideas explored in the discussion are based on principles which should support the construction of all learning experiences to ensure they benefit all children. That is, in this last instance, with the discussion of personalized learning, we can see how because it is fundamentally a good way to design learning, it is an activity that encourages achievement for all children. And this can be said for most of the discussions throughout this book. While specific ideas and examples of good practice with regard to supporting children's learning have been discussed, with reference to the particular issues being explored in any one chapter, the truth is that any learning activity that takes account of diversity, and provides equal opportunities for learning will benefit the learning of all children.

What the diversity, equality and achievement debate has served to do is raise awareness of what constitutes good learning for particular groups of children, and this has, by default, often improved the learning experiences of all children. Essentially, where you seek to develop your professional practice to improve your ability to provide motivating and interesting learning experiences for children, whatever prompts you to begin your research into how you can meet the needs of particular children you work with, your whole practice as a professional will become better developed. You may have picked up this book because you wanted to know more about working with children from a cultural background different to your own, or children who are a different gender to you, or are differently-abled to you but whatever your reason for reading this book, or parts of it, the skills, knowledge and understanding you will have explored will have a positive impact on your work with all children, whatever their culture, ethnicity, gender, class or background.

# Bibliography

Adams, M., Bell, L.A. and Griffin, P. (ed.) (2007) *Teaching for Diversity and Social Justice*, 2nd edn. New York and London: Routledge.

Anderson, A. (2004) 'Resilience', in R. Hamilton and D. Moore (eds) (2004) *Educational Interventions for Refugee Children: Theoretical Perspectives and Implementing Best Practice*. Abingdon: Routledge.

Arnot, M. and Mac an Ghaill, M. (2006) *Gender and Education*. Abingdon: Routledge.

Aspinall, P. and Watters, C. (2010) *Refugees and Asylum Seekers: A Review from an Equality and Human Rights Perspective*. Manchester: Equality and Human Rights Commission. Available at: http://www.equalityhumanrights.com/uploaded_files/research/refugees_and_asylum_seekers_research_report.pdf

Baker, C. (ed.) (2001) *Bilingual Education and Bilingualism, 27: Foundations of Bilingual Education and Bilingualism*. Bristol: Multilingual Matters Limited.

Baker, L. and Credland, S. (ed.) (2004) *Listen Up: The Voices of Homeless Children*. London: Shelter.

Barker, R. (1997) *Political Ideas in Modern Britain: In and After the 20th Century*. London: Routledge.

BBC (1999) 'Health: Disabled Complain of Widespread Bullying'. Available at: http://news.bbc.co.uk/1/hi/health/371638.stm (accessed 30.03.10).

BBC (2003) 'Boys Guilty of Killing "Gypsy"'. Available at: http://news.bbc.co.uk/1/hi/england/merseyside/3246518.stm (accessed February 2010).

BBC (2006) 'The EU's Baby Blues'. Available at: www.news.bbc.co.uk/1/hi/world/europe/4768644.stm (accessed 22.03.10).

BBC (2009a) 'Karl Marx'. Available at: www.bbc.co.uk/history/historic_figures/marx_karl.shtml (accessed 29.07.09).

BBC (2009b) 'Murder Mother's Abuse "Ignored"'. Available at: http://news.bbc.co.uk/1/hi/england/leicestershire/8263027.stm (accessed 30.03.10).

BBC (2010) 'Becoming a Step-parent'. Available at: www.bbc.co.uk/parenting/family_matters/step_becoming.shtml (accessed 22.03.10).

Beales, D. (2005) *Enlightenment and Reform in Eighteenth-Century Europe*. London: I.B. Tauris & Co Ltd.

Bell, D. (2009) mentioned in E. Taylor, D. Gillborn and G. Ladson-Billings (eds) (2009) *Foundations of Critical Race Theory in Education*. Abingdon: Routledge.

Bellamy, R. (ed.) (2003) *Political Concepts*. Manchester: Manchester University Press.

Benson, J. (2003) *The Working Class in Britain, 1850–1939*. London: I.B. Tauris & Co Ltd.

Bhopal, K. and Myers, M. (2008) *Insiders, Outsiders and Others: Gypsies and Identity*. Hatfield: University of Hertfordshire Press.

Bhopal, K., Gundara, J., Jones, C. and Owen, C. (2000) *Working Towards Inclusive Education: Aspects of Good Practice for Gypsy Traveller Pupils*. DfEE Research Report No. 238. Norwich: DfEE.

Bird, C. (1999) *The Myth of Liberal Individualism.* Cambridge: Cambridge University Press.

Blastland, M. (2008) 'Just what is Average?' Available at: http://news.bbc.co.uk/1/hi/magazine/7581120.stm (accessed 28.10.09).

Bonnett, A. (2000) *White Identities.* Harlow: Pearson.

Braudy, L. (2005) *From Chivalry to Terrorism: War and the Changing Nature of Masculinity.* Westminster, MD: Alfred A. Knopf Incorporated.

Browne, N. (1987) 'Do the Gentlemen in Whitehall Know Best? An Historical Perspective of Pre-school Provision in Britain', in N. Browne and P. France (eds), *Untying the Apron Strings Anti-sexist Provision for the Under Fives.* Milton Keynes: Open University Press. pp. 8–31.

Browne, N. and France, P. (1986a) '"Only Cissies Wear Dresses": A Look at Sexist Talk in the Nursery', in N. Browne and P. France (eds), *Untying the Apron Strings: Anti-sexist Provision for the Under Fives.* Milton Keynes: Open University Press. pp. 146–59.

Browne, N. and France, P. (eds) (1986b) *Untying the Apron Strings: Anti-sexist Provision for the Under Fives.* Milton Keynes: Open University Press.

Cabinet Office Social Exclusion Task Force (2008) *Aspiration and Attainment Amongst Young People in Deprived Communities. Analysis and Discussion Paper.* London: Social Exclusion Task Force.

Cannadine, D. (2000) *Class in Britain.* London: Penguin.

Centre for Analysis of Social Exclusion (2010) *An Anatomy of Economic Inequality in the UK – Summary Report of the National Equality Panel.* Government Equalities Office.

Chambers, D. (2001) *Representing the Family.* London: Sage.

Chara, K.A. (2005) *A Safe Place for Caleb: An Interactive Book for Kids, Teens and Adults with Issues of Attachment, Grief, Loss, or Early Trauma.* London: Jessica Kingsley Publishers.

Charlesworth, S.J. (2000) *Phenomenology of Working Class Experience.* Cambridge: Cambridge University Press.

Children's Rights Director for England (2009) *Care and Prejudice: A Report of Children's Experience.* London: Ofsted.

Cole, W.O and Sambhi, P.S. (1978) *The Sikhs, their Religious Beliefs and Practices.* London: Routledge and Kegan Paul Ltd.

Daiute, C. (ed.) (2006) *International Perspectives on Youth Conflict and Development.* Oxford: Oxford University Press.

Deater-Deckard, K. (2004) *Parenting Stress.* New Haven, CT: Yale University Press.

Delgado, R. and Stefancic, J. (2001) *Critical Race Theory: An Introduction.* New York: New York University Press.

Department for Children, Schools and Families (DCSF) (2007a) *Guidance on the Duty to Promote Community Cohesion.* Nottingham: DCSF Publications.

Department for Children, Schools and Families (DCSF) (2007b) *The Children's Plan.* Nottingham: DCSF Publications. Available at: http://www.dcsf.gov.uk/childrensplan/ (accessed 30.03.10).

Department for Children, Schools and Families (DCSF) (2009a) *Building Futures: Developing Trust: A Focus on Provision for Children from Gypsy, Roma and Traveller Backgrounds in Early Years Foundation Stage.* Nottingham: DCSF Publications. Available at: www.standards.dcsf.gov.uk

Department for Children, Schools and Families (DCSF) (2009b) *Common Core of Skills and Knowledge*. Nottingham: DCSF Publications.

Department for Children, Schools and Families (DCSF) (2009c) *Gender and Education Mythbusters: Addressing Gender and Achievement Myths and Realities*. Nottingham: DCSF Publications.

Department for Children, Schools and Families (DCSF) (2009d) *Moving Forward Together: Raising Gypsy, Roma and Traveller Achievement. Booklet 1: Introduction*. Nottingham: DCSF Publications. Available at: www.standards.dcsf.gov.uk

Department for Children, Schools and Families (DCSF) (2009e) *Moving Forward Together: Raising Gypsy, Roma and Traveller Achievement. Booklet 2: Leadership and Management*. Nottingham: DCSF Publications. Available at: www.standards .dcsf.gov.uk

Department for Children, Schools and Families (DCSF) (2009f) *Moving Forward Together: Raising Gypsy, Roma and Traveller Achievement. Booklet 3: Learning and Teaching*. Nottingham: DCSF Publications. Available at: www.standards. dcsf.gov.uk

Department for Children, Schools and Families (DCSF) (2009g) *Moving Forward Together: Raising Gypsy, Roma and Traveller Achievement. Booklet 4: Engagement with Parents, Carers and the Wider Community*. Nottingham: DCSF Publications. Available at: www.standards.dcsf.gov.uk

Department for Children, Schools and Families (DCSF) (2009h) *Improving the Educational Attainment of Children in Care (Looked After Children)*. Nottingham: DCSF Publications.

Department for Children, Schools and Families (DCSF) (2009i) *Make Them Go Away*. Nottingham: DCSF Publications.

Department for Children, Schools and Families (DCSF) (2010a) *Gender and Achievement*. Nottingham: DCSF Publications. Available at: http://national-strategies.standards.dcsf.gov.uk (accessed 24.04.10).

Department for Children, Schools and Families (DCSF) (2010b) *Key Stage 4 Attainment by Pupil Characteristics, in England 2008/09*. www.dcsf.gov.uk/ rsgateway/DB/SFR/s000900/SFR34_2009Revised.pdf (accessed 24.03.10).

Department for Education and Skills (DfES) (2001) *Special Educational Needs: Code of Practice*. Annesley, Nottinghamshire: DfES.

Department for Education and Skills (DfES) (2003) *Aiming High: Raising the Achievement of Minority Ethnic Pupils*. Annesley, Nottinghamshire: DfES.

Department for Education and Skills (DfES) (2004a) *Removing Barriers to Achievement*. Annesley, Nottinghamshire: DfES.

Department for Education and Skills (DfES) (2004b) *Aiming High: Guidance on Supporting the Education of Asylum Seeking and Refugee Children*. Annesley, Nottinghamshire: DfES.

Department for Education and Skills (DfES) (2004c) *Every Child Matters*. Annesley, Nottinghamshire: DfES.

Department for Education and Skills (DfES) (2005) *Ensuring the Attainment of White Working Class Boys in Writing*. Annesley, Nottinghamshire: DfES. Available at: http://nationalstrategies.standards.dcsf.gov.uk/node/97547 (accessed 05.08.09).

Department for Education and Skills (DfES) (2006a) *Ethnicity and Education: The Evidence on Minority Ethnic Pupils aged 5–16*. Annesley, Nottinghamshire: DfES.

Department for Education and Skills (DfES) (2006b) *Priority Review: Exclusion of Black Pupils 'Getting it. Getting it right'.* Annesley, Nottinghamshire: DfES. Available at: http://www.standards.dfes.gov.uk/ethnicminorities/resources/PriorityReview Sept06.pdf (accessed on January 2010).

Department for Education and Skills (DfES) (2006c) *Implementing the Disability Discrimination Act in Schools and Early Years Settings.* Annesley, Nottinghamshire: DfES.

Derrrington, C. (2004) 'ITE Session: Gypsy, Roma, Travellers'. Available at www. multiverse.ac.uk (accessed February 2010).

Derrington, C. (2005) 'ITE Session: On the Margins: Racism and Gypsy Traveller Communities'. Available at www.multiverse.ac.uk (accessed February 2010).

Derrington, C. and Kendall, S. (2004) *Gypsy Traveller Children in Secondary Schools.* Stoke-on-Trent: Trentham.

Di Ciacco, J. (2008) *The Colors of Grief: Understanding a Child's Journey through Loss from Birth to Adulthood.* London and Philadelphia, PA: Jessica Kingsley Publishers.

Disability Rights Commission (2005) *Code of Practice for Schools.* London: TSO.

Disability Rights Commission (2010a) *Doing the Duty: An Overview of the Disability Equality Duty for the Public Sector.* Available at: http://www.dothed-uty.org/ (accessed 29.03.10).

Disability Rights Commission (2010b) *The Disability Equality Duty: Guidance on Gathering and Analysing Evidence to Inform Action.* Available at: http://www. dotheduty.org/files/DRC_Evidence_Gathering_Guidance.pdf

Dockett, K.H. (ed.) (2003) *Psychology and Buddhism: From Individual to Global Community.* New York: Kluwer Academic/Plenum Publishers.

Du Gay, P. (ed.) (1997) *Production of Culture/Cultures of Production.* London: Sage in association with The Open University.

Dunlop, A-W. (2006) *Informing Transitions in the Early Years.* Maidenhead: Open University Press.

Elias, N. (2001) *The Society of Individuals.* New York and London: Continuum International Publishing.

Empson, J. (2004) *Atypical Child Development in Context.* Basingstoke: Palgrave Macmillan.

Epstein, D. (1993) *Changing Classroom Cultures: Anti-racism, Politics and Schools.* Stoke-on-Trent: Trentham.

Featherstone, B. (2004) *Family Life and Family Support: A Feminist Analysis.* Basingstoke: Palgrave Macmillan.

Foley, P., Roche, J. and Tucker, S. (eds) (2001) *Children in Society: Contemporary Theory, Policy and Practice.* Basingstoke: Palgrave in association with The Open University.

Fox, R. (2009) 'The Plight of Europe's Roma', *The Guardian.* Available at: http://www.guardian.co.uk/commentisfree/2009/jun/22/roma-europe-discrimination-attacks

Francis, B. and Skelton, C. (2001) *Investigating Gender Contemporary Perspectives in Education.* Buckingham: The Open University Press.

Gaine, C. (2001) '"If It's Not Hurting It's Not Working": Teaching Teachers About "Race"', *Research Papers in Education* 16(1): 93–113.

Gaine, C. (2005) *We're All White Thanks: The Persisting Myth about 'White' Schools*. Stoke-on-Trent: Trentham Books.

Gaine, C. and George, R. (1999) *Gender, 'Race' and Class in Schooling: A New Introduction*. London: Falmer Press.

Garner, S. (2010) *Racisms: An Introduction*. London: Sage.

Garrett, B. (1998) *Personal Identity and Self-Consciousness*. London: Routledge.

Gillborn, G. (2008) *Racism and Education: Coincidence or Conspiracy*. Abingdon: Routledge.

Gillborn, G. (2009) Interview about his book *Racism and Education: Coincidence or Conspiracy*. Available at: http://www.informaworld.com/smpp/education-arena_interviewarchive_interview3~db=all (accessed September 2009).

Gillborn, D. and Gipps, C. (1996) *Recent Research on the Achievements of Ethnic Minority Pupils*. London: Ofsted.

Gillborn, D. and Mirza, H. (2000) *Educational Inequality: Mapping Race, Class and Gender*. London: Ofsted. Available at: http://www.ofsted.gov.uk/Ofsted-home/Publications-and-research/Browse-all-by/Education/Inclusion/Minority-ethnic-children/Educational-inequality-mapping-race-class-and-gender (accessed 05.08.09).

Hamilton, R. and Moore, D. (2004) *Educational Interventions for Refugee Children: Theoretical Perspectives and Implementing Best Practice*. London: RoutledgeFalmer.

Hannon, C. (2009) 'Getting Used to Gay Parents'. Available at: www.guardian.co.uk/commentisfree/2009/nov/27/gay-parents-child-development (accessed 22.03.10).

Hargreaves, J. (2004) 'From History to Her Story: Yorkshire Women's Lives On-line 1100 to The Present'. Available at: http://www.historytoherstory.org.uk/index.php?nextcount=1&targetid=15&themeid=5 (accessed 24.04.10).

Harris, C.I. (1993) 'Whiteness as Property', *Harvard Law Review* 106(8): 1710–91.

Her Majesty's Government (1998) *Human Rights Act 1998*. London: The Stationery Office.

Her Majesty's Government (2004a) *Children Act 2004: Explanatory Notes*. London: The Stationery Office.

Her Majesty's Government (2004b) *The Human Rights Act 1998 (Amendment) Order 2004*. London: The Stationery Office.

Her Majesty's Government (2006) *Racial and Religious Hatred Act 2006*. London: The Stationery Office.

Heydt, C. (2006) *Rethinking Mill's Ethics*. London: Continuum International Publishing.

Hills, J. (2004) *Inequality and the State*. Oxford: Oxford University Press.

Hinman, L.M. (2003) *Ethics: A Pluralist Approach to Moral Theory*, 3rd edn. Belmont: Wadsworth Publishing.

Ivinson, G. and Murphy, P. (2007) *Rethinking Single-Sex Teaching*. Maidenhead: Open University Press.

Jones, C. (1999) *Poverty, Welfare and the Disciplinary State*. London: Routledge.

Jones, R. (1999) *Teaching Racsim or Tackling it? Multicultural Stories from Beginning White Teachers*. Stoke-on-Trent: Trentham.

Kehily, M.J. (ed.) (2007) *Understanding Youth: Perspectives, Identities and Practices*. London: Sage in association with The Open University.

King, J.E. (2004) 'Dysconscious Racism: Ideology, Identity and the Miseducation of Teachers', in G. Ladson-Billings and D. Gillborn (eds) *The RoutledgeFalmer Reader in Multicultural Education*. Abingdon: RoutledgeFalmer, pp. 71–83.

Knowles, G. (ed.) (2006) *Supporting Inclusive Practice*. London: David Fulton.

Knowles, G. (2009) *Ensuring Every Child Matters*. London: Sage.

Knowles, G. (ed.) (2010) *Supporting Inclusive Practice*, 2nd edn. Abingdon: Routledge.

Korostelina, K. (2007) *Social Identity and Conflict*. Gordonsville, VA: Palgrave Macmillan.

Kumria, M. (1987) 'Establishing Co-operation between Parents and Staff: A Parent's View', in N. Browne and P. France (eds) *Untying the Apron Strings: Anti-sexist Provision for the Under Fives*. Milton Keynes: Open University Press. pp. 68–88.

Laird, E. (2007) *Kiss the Dust*. London: Macmillan Children's Books.

Lamb, B. (2009) *Lamb Inquiry: Special Educational Needs and Parental Confidence*. London: DCSF.

Lawler, S. (2009) *Identity: Sociological Perspectives*. Cambridge: Polity Press.

Lawrence, D. (2006) *And Still I Rise: Seeking Justice for Stephen*. London: Faber and Faber.

Leonardo, Z. (2002) 'The Souls of White Folk: Critical Pedagogy, Whiteness Studies and Globalization Discourse', *Race, Ethnicity and Education* 5(1): 29–50.

Leonardo, Z. (2005) *Critical Pedagogy and Race*. Malden, MA: Blackwell.

Litosseliti, L. (ed.) (2002) *Gender Identity and Discourse Analysis*. Philadelphia, PA: John Benjamins Publishing Company.

Lund, B. (2002) *Understanding the Welfare State: Social Justice or Social Exclusion?* London: Sage.

Macpherson, W. (1999) *The Stephen Lawrence Inquiry: Report of an Inquiry by Sir William Macpherson of Cluny*. London: Home Office. Available from: http://www.archive.official-documents.co.uk/document/cm42/4262/4262.htm

Madigan, J.H. (2007) *Truth, Politics, and Universal Human Rights*. Gordonsville, VA: Palgrave Macmillan.

Marx, S. (2006) *Revealing the Invisible: Confronting Passive Racism in Teacher Education*. New York: Routledge.

Mayseless, O. (2002) *Parenting Representations: Theory, Research, and Clinical Implications*. Cambridge: Cambridge University Press.

McAll, C. (1992) *Class, Ethnicity and Social Inequality*. Montreal, QC: McGill-Queen's University Press.

McIntosh, P. (1990) 'White Privilege: Unpacking the Invisible Knapsack', *Independent School*, Winter, pp. 31–6.

McIntyre, A. (1997) *Making Meaning of Whiteness: Exploring Racial Identity with White Teachers*. Albany: State University of New York Press.

Mencap (1999) *Living in Fear*. Available at: www.mencap.org.uk

Mensah, F.K. and Kiernan, K.E. (2010) 'Gender Differences in Educational Attainment: Influences of the Family Environment', *British Educational Research Journal* 36(2): 239–60.

Mirza, H.S. (2009) *Race, Gender and Educational Desire: Why Black Women Succeed and Fail*. Abingdon: Routledge.

Mongon, D. and Chapman, C. (2008) *Successful Leadership for Promoting the Achievement of White Working Class Pupils.* University of Manchester for The National Union of Teachers and National College for School Leadership.

Multiverse (2009) 'Hidden Identities in the Staffroom: Being a Gypsy and a Teacher'. Available at: http://www.multiverse.ac.uk/viewarticle2.aspx?contentId=15044 (accessed February 2010).

Nash, P. (2008) *We Are All Middle Class Now.* Available at: teachersupport.info/news/seced/Seced-03-6-2008.php (accessed 29.07.09).

National Children's Bureau (2009) *What is the Disabled Children's Manifesto for Change?* Available at: www.ncb.org.uk/ (accessed 29.03.10).

National Society for the Prevention of Cruelty to Children (NSPCC) (2010) 'Sexual Abuse'. http://www.nspcc.org.uk/helpandadvice/whatchildabuse/sexualabuse/sexualabuse_wda36370.html (accessed 24.03.10).

Niemöller, M., Pastor (n.d.) http://www.dpjs.co.uk/white/theycameforme.html (accessed 05.01.10).

Nishi Bolakee (2006) www.bbc.co.uk/1/hi/business/5040140.stm (accessed 20.02.10).

O'Donnell, M. and Sharpe, S. (2000) *Uncertain Masculinities.* London and New York: Routledge.

Office for National Statistics (2009) *Standard Occupational Classification 2000.* Available at: http://www.ons.gov.uk/about-statistics/classifications/current/SOC2000/about-soc2000/index.html (accessed 18.08.09).

Office for National Statistics (n.d.) General Population Statistics. Available at: http://www.statistics.gov.uk/cci/nugget.asp?id=263&Pos=1&ColRank=2&Rank=256 (accessed January 2010).

Ofra, M. (ed.) (2002) *Parenting Representations: Theory, Research, and Clinical Implications.* Cambridge: Cambridge University Press.

Office for Standards in Education (Ofsted) (2003a) *Boys' Achievement in Secondary Schools.* London: Ofsted Publications Centre.

Office for Standards in Education (Ofsted) (2003b) *Provision and Support for Traveller Pupils.* London: Ofsted. Available at: www.ofsted.gov.uk

Office for Standards in Education (Ofsted) (2005a) *English 2000–05.* London: Ofsted.

Office for Standards in Education (Ofsted) (2005b) *Informing Practice in English.* London: Ofsted.

Office for Standards in Education (Ofsted) (2006) *Inclusion: Does it Matter Where Children are Taught?* Her Majesty's Inspectors 2535.

Office for Standards in Education (Ofsted) (2007) *Early Years: Getting on Well: Enjoying, Achieving and Contributing.* London: Ofsted.

Office for Standards in Education (Ofsted) (2008a) *Ofsted Disability Equality Scheme.* London: Ofsted.

Office for Standards in Education (Ofsted) (2008b) *Children's Care Monitor 2008: Children's Views on How Care is Doing: A Report by the Children's Rights Director.* London: Ofsted.

Office for Standards in Education (Ofsted) (2008c) *White Boys from Low-income Backgrounds: Good Practice in Schools.* London: Ofsted.

Office for Standards in Education (Ofsted) (n.d.) RAISEonline. Available at: http://www.ofsted.gov.uk/Ofsted-home/About-us/FAQs/RAISEonline2 (accessed 07.01.10).

Oppenheim, D. (ed.) (2007) *Attachment Theory in Clinical Work with Children: Bridging the Gap between Research and Practice.* New York: The Guilford Press.

Ossowski, S. (1998) *Class Structure in the Social Consciousness*. London: Routledge.

Paechter, C. (2001) 'Using Poststructuralist Ideas in Gender Theory and Research', in B. Francis and C. Skelton (eds) *Investigating Gender: Contemporary Perspectives in Education*. Buckingham: Open University Press. pp. 41–51.

Parekh, B. (2000) *The Future of Multi-Ethnic Britain: The Parekh Report*. London: Profile Books.

Parekh, B. (2008) *A New Politics of Identity*. Basingstoke: Palgrave Macmillan.

Pennington, D.C. (2000) *Social Cognition*. London: Routledge.

Preston, G. (2008) *2 Skint 4 School*. London: Child Poverty Action Group.

Prior, V. (2006) *Understanding Attachment and Attachment Disorders: Theory, Evidence and Practice*. London: Jessica Kingsley Publishers.

QCDA (2010a) http://curriculum.qcda.gov.uk/new-primary-curriculum/areas-of-learning/understanding-English-communication-and-languages/programme-of-learning/index.aspx?tab=2 (accessed 01.02.10).

QCDA (2010b) *Supporting Looked-after Children*. Available at: www.curriculum.qcda.gov.uk/key-stages-3-and-4/case_studies/casestudieslibrary/case-studies/Supporting_looked-after_children.aspx (accessed 24.03.10).

QCDA (2010c) *The National Curriculum Primary Handbook*. Coventry: QCDA. Race Relations Amendment Act 2000. Available at: http://www.opsi.gov.uk/acts/acts2000/ukpga_20000034_en_1 (accessed January 2010).

RAISEonline (2010) https://www.raiseonline.org/login.aspx?ReturnUrl=%2findex.aspx (accessed 07.01.10).

Rennison, N. (2001) *Sigmund Freud*. Harpenden: Pocket Essentials.

ReoCities (n.d.) 'Patrin: A Brief History of the Roma'. Available at: www.reocities.com/~patrin/history.htm (accessed February 2010).

Reumann, M.G. (2005) *American Sexual Character: Sex, Gender, and National Identity in the Kinsey Reports*. Berkeley and Los Angeles: University of California Press.

Rice, B. and Savage, T. (2006) *Against the Odds*. London: Shelter.

Richardson, B. (2005) *Tell It Like It Is: How our Schools Fail Black Children*. London: Bookmark; Stoke-on-Trent: Trentham Books.

Richardson, R. (1990) *Daring to be a Teacher*. Stoke-on-Trent: Trentham Books.

Richardson, R. (2004) *Here, There and Everywhere*. Stoke-on-Trent: Trentham Books.

Richman, N. (1998) *In The Midst of the Whirlwind: A Manual for Helping Refugee Children*. Stoke-on-Trent: Trentham Books.

Riddell, M. (1998) *Statisticians Tell Us That We're All Middle Class Now – But That Doesn't Stop Poorer People Dying Younger*. Available at: http://www.newstatesman.com/199812040008 (accessed 02.01.10).

Robb. M. (2001) 'The Changing Experiences of Childhood', in P. Foley, J. Roche and S. Tucker (eds) (2001) *Children in Society: Contemporary Theory, Policy and Practice*. Basingstoke: Palgrave in association with The Open University.

Roosevelt, T.R., Jr. (2005) *Building on the Promise of Diversity: How We Can Move to the Next Level in Our Workplaces, Our Communities, and Our Society*. Saranac Lake, NY: AMACOM.

Rutter, J. (2003) *Supporting Refugee Children in 21st Century Britain: A Compendium of Essential Information*. Stoke-on-Trent: Trentham Books.

Rutter, J. (2006) *Refugee Children in the UK*. Maidenhead: Open University Press.

Ryde, J. (2009) *Being White in the Helping Professions*. London: Jessica Kingsley Publishers.

Skelton, C. and Francis, B. (eds) (2003) *Boys and Girls in the Primary Classroom*. Buckingham: Open University Press.

Skelton, C., Francis, B. and Valkanova, Y. (2007) *Breaking Down the Stereotypes: Gender and Achievement in Schools*. Manchester: Equal Opportunities Commission.

Smith, E. (2005) *Analysing Underachievement in Schools*. London: Continuum International Publishing.

Smith, M.K. (2009) *'Race' and Difference – Developing Practice in Lifelong Learning*. Available at: http://www.infed.org/lifelonglearning/b-race.htm (accessed January 2010).

Social Policy (2008) *Social Policy in the UK: The Poor Law*. www2.rgu.ac.uk/publicpolicy/introduction (accessed 5 September 2010).

Solomon, R.P., Portelli, J.P., Daniel, B. and Campbell, A. (2005) 'The Discourse of Denial: How White Teacher Candidates Construct Race, Racism and "White Privilege"', *Race, Ethnicity and Education* 8(2): 147–69.

Stobbs, P. (2008) *Extending Inclusion – Access for Disabled Children and Young People to Extended Schools and Children's Centres: A Development Manual*. Department for Children, Schools and Families and the Council for Disabled Children.

Stuart-Hamilton, I. (1996) *Key Ideas in Psychology*. London: Jessica Kingsley Publishers.

Tasker, F. (2005) 'Lesbian Mothers, Gay Fathers, and Their Children: A Review', *Journal of Developmental & Behavioral Pediatrics* 26(3): 224–40.

Tatum, B. (1999) *'Why Are All the Black Kids Sitting Together in the Cafeteria?' And Other Conversations About Race*. New York: Basic Books.

Taylor, E., Gillborn, D. and Ladson-Billings, G. (eds) (2009) *Foundations of Critical Race Theory in Education*. Abingdon: Routledge.

The Poverty Site (2009) http://www.poverty.org.uk/summary/key%20facts.shtml (accessed 02.12.09).

The Swann Report (1985) *Education for All. Report of the Committee of Enquiry into the Education of Children from Minority Ethnic Groups*. Available at: http://www.educationengland.org.uk/documents/swann (accessed on 26 February 2010).

Thompson, J. (2000) *Women, Class and Education*. London: Routledge.

Thompson, B. (2006) 'Reviewing Gender Issues in the Primary classroom' in G. Knowles, *Supporting Inclusive Practice*. London: David Fulton.

Thompson, R. (2007) 'Belonging', in M.J. Kehily (ed.) (2007) *Understanding Youth: Perspectives, Identities and Practices*. London: Sage in association with The Open University, pp. 147–80.

Thomson, K. (ed.) (2003) *British Social Attitudes – The 20th Report: Continuity and Change over Two Decades*. London: Sage.

Tierney, S. (2007) (ed.) *Accommodating Cultural Diversity*. Abingdon: Ashgate Publishing Ltd.

Tomalin, C. (1992) *The Life and Death of Mary Wollstonecraft*. London: Penguin Books.

Traber, D. (2007) *Whiteness, Otherness and the Individualism Paradox from Huck to Punk*. Basingstoke: Palgrave Macmillan.

Training and Development Agency (2008) *Professional Standards for Qualified Teacher Status and Requirements for Initial Teacher Training (Revised 2008)*. London: TDA.

United Nations High Commissioner for Refugees (UNHCR) (2007) *The 1951 Refugee Convention: Questions and Answers*. Geneva: UNHCR Media and Public Information Services.

Walsh, F. (2006) *Strengthening Family Resilience*. New York: The Guilford Press.

Waterman, B. (2003) *The Birth of an Adoptive, Foster or Stepmother: Beyond Biological Mothering Attachments*. London: Jessica Kingsley Publishers.

Weedon, C. (2004) *Identity and Culture: Narratives of Difference and Belonging*. Maidenhead: Open University Press.

Weiner, G. (1985) *Just a Bunch of Girls*. Buckingham: Open University Press.

Westwood, P. (2007) *Commonsense Methods for Children with Special Educational Needs*, 5th edn. London: Routledge.

Wheen, F. (2000) *Karl Marx*. London: Fourth Estate.

Wikstrom, Per-Olof H. (2006) *Adolescent Crime: Individual Differences and Lifestyles*. Uffculme, Devon: Willan Publishing.

Wilkins, A., Derrington, C., Foster, B., White, R. and Martin, K. (2009) *Improving Educational Outcomes for Gypsy, Roma and Traveller Pupils. What Works? Contextual Influences and Constructive Conditions that Influence Pupils. Achievement Research Report DCSF-RR170*. Available at: www.dcsf.gov.uk/research (accessed February 2010).

Wright, E.O. (2000) *Class Counts*. New York: Cambridge University Press.

Zephaniah, B. (2001) *Refugee Boy*. London: Bloomsbury.

## Websites

www.communitycare.co.uk/Articles/2007/10/24/106206/frequent-care-placements may-lead-to-crime-research-finds.htm (accessed 25.03.10).

www.family-lawfirm.co.uk/Articles/Children/Step-parents-rights-and-responsibilities.aspx

# Index

Added to a page number 'f' denotes a figure and 't' denotes a table.

# CHANGING BEHAVIOUR IN SCHOOLS

## Promoting Positive Relationships and Wellbeing

**Sue Roffey** *University of Western Sydney and University College London*

Good teachers know that positive relationships with students and school connectedness lead to both improved learning and better behaviour for all students, and this is backed up by research. This book will show you how to promote positive behaviour and wellbeing in your setting.

Taking an holistic approach to working with students, the author provides examples of effective strategies for encouraging prosocial and collaborative behaviour in the classroom, the school and the wider community. Chapters look at the importance of the social and emotional aspects of learning, and ways to facilitate change.

Issues covered include:

• developing a sense of belonging in the classroom
• teaching approaches that maximize engagement and participation
• how to respond effectively to challenging situations
• ways to re-engage with students who have become marginalized.

Each chapter has case studies from primary and secondary schools, activities, checklists and suggestions for further reading.

READERSHIP
Trainee teachers and newly qualified teachers

**November 2010 • 232 pages**
**Cloth (978-1-84920-077-6) • £65.00**
**Paper (978-1-84920-078-3) • £20.99**

# ALSO FROM SAGE

# CHILDREN'S RIGHTS IN PRACTICE

Edited by **Phil Jones** *University of Leeds* and
**Gary Walker** *Leeds Metropolitan University*

Considering the rights of the child is now central
to all fields involving children and to good multi-
agency working. This book offers an explana-
tion of the theoretical issues and the key policy
developments that are crucial to all professions,
and helps the reader to understand children's
rights in relation to their role in working with children and young people. Looking at education,
health, social care and welfare, it bridges the gap
between policy and practice for children from Birth
to 19 years.  Chapters cover:
- the child's right to play
- youth justice, children's rights and the voice of the child
- ethical dilemmas in different contexts
- involvement, participation and decision making
- safeguarding and child protection, social justice and exclusion.

This book helps the reader understand what constitutes good practice, whilst
considering the advantages and tensions involved in working across disciplines
to implement children's rights against a complex legislative and social policy
backdrop.

April 2011 • 256 pages
Cloth (978-1-84920-379-1) • £65.00
Paper (978-1-84920-380-7) • £22.99

**ALSO FROM SAGE**

978-1-84860-616-6

978-1-84920-030-1

978-1-84920-114-8

978-1-84860-713-2

978-1-84920-076-9

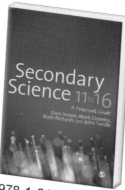

978-1-84920-126-1

978-1-84920-078-3

Find out more about these titles and our wide range
of books for education students and practitioners at
**www.sagepub.co.uk/education**

**EXCITING EDUCATION TEXTS FROM SAGE**